The Heart of the Hereafter

Love Stories from the End of Life

The Heart of the Hereafter

Love Stories from the End of Life

Marcia Brennan, Ph.D.

AXIS MUNDI
BOOKS

Winchester, UK
Washington, USA

First published by Axis Mundi Books, 2014
Axis Mundi Books is an imprint of John Hunt Publishing Ltd., Laurel House, Station Approach,
Alresford, Hants, SO24 9JH, UK
office1@jhpbooks.net
www.johnhuntpublishing.com
www.axismundi-books.com

For distributor details and how to order please visit the 'Ordering' section on our website.

Text copyright: Marcia Brennan 2013

ISBN: 978 1 78279 528 5

A CIP catalogue record for this book is available from the British Library.

Design: Stuart Davies
www.stuartdaviesart.com

Printed and bound by CPI Group (UK) Ltd, Croydon, CR0 4YY

We operate a distinctive and ethical publishing philosophy in all
areas of our business, from our global network of authors to
production and worldwide distribution.

CONTENTS

Also by Marcia Brennan:

Words Beyond Words: Finding Language at the End of Life. Bristol, UK: Intellect Books and the University of Chicago Press, forthcoming.

The Angels In Between: The Book of Muse. Winchester, UK: Axis Mundi Books, 2013.

The Day Your Heart Broke In Your Eyes. Nevada City, CA: Blue Dolphin Publishing, 2011.

Curating Consciousness: Mysticism and the Modern Museum. Cambridge, MA and London: MIT Press, 2010.

Flowering Light: Kabbalistic Mysticism and the Art of Elliot R. Wolfson. Houston: Rice University Press, 2009.

Modernism's Masculine Subjects: Matisse, the New York School, and Post-Painterly Abstraction. Cambridge, MA and London: MIT Press, 2004.

Painting Gender, Constructing Theory: The Alfred Stieglitz Circle and American Formalist Aesthetics. Cambridge, MA and London: MIT Press, 2001.

For Dr. Eduardo Bruera
and all the members of his marvelous team who,
every day, practice both the heart and the humanity
of palliative care

And the glorious beauty shall be a fading flower
—Isaiah 28.4

Acknowledgements

One evening, my dear friend Dr. Jennifer Wheler and I were having a quiet dinner together at one of our favorite neighborhood restaurants. Jennifer is an oncologist and an Assistant Professor of Investigational Cancer Therapeutics at the M. D. Anderson Cancer Center. She is also the founder of COLLAGE: The Art for Cancer Network, a nonprofit organization dedicated to providing innovative art programs for people living with cancer. For well over a year, I watched the organization's activities with admiration. Yet on that particular evening, I knew in my heart that something had changed. As usual, we were discussing our work. I had just completed the writing of one of my art historical monographs, and I had sent the finished manuscript to the publisher earlier that week. As we celebrated this development, I heard myself say to her, "I think you should trigger the paperwork for the credentialing process for the Artist In Residence program, so that I can come work at M. D. Anderson through COLLAGE." Knowing very well that I had not worked in a hospital since my early days as a teenager volunteering on the pediatrics ward of a local hospital, Jennifer looked over at me carefully and asked, *"Are you sure?"* Not only did I say yes, but I knew that I wanted to work with people at the end of life. This turned out to be one of the best decisions I ever made. Just as COLLAGE's programming is inspired by a belief in the transformative power of art, in turn, it is not possible to undertake such work oneself and not have it transform your own life, in ways that are all for the better. After doing this work for a few years, I began writing a scholarly study describing my experiences. This book is entitled *Words Beyond Words: Finding Language at the End of Life*. As I wrote the text, I repeatedly found myself thinking what a shame it was that a selection of the beautiful end of life stories could not be presented in a brief, accessible format for a general audience. This led me to realize that a book had emerged within a book, the result of which is this little volume, *The Heart of the Hereafter*. As you read the stories in this small book, please keep in mind that none of these experiences would have been possible were it not for Jennifer Wheler's extraordinary vision and initiative. I am also grateful to COLLAGE's Executive Director, Marcel Bartolazzi Lake, for all that she does, and for doing it all so gracefully. When I initially began this work, I partnered with the painter Lynn Randolph, and on so many occasions I watched as she skillfully produced lovely and moving images for the patients. My admiration goes to her and to all of the talented visual artists who work with COLLAGE.

Much like the stories that appear in this volume, the writing of this book itself represents an act of love that involves the talents, efforts, and generosity of many people. Working on a Palliative Care Unit is inherently a team effort, and every person there has been my teacher. Nowhere is this more the case than with the nursing staff who administer the actual bedside care for the patients. I would like to thank Marisa Beck, Chanelle Clerc, Pilar Durias, Marysela Guerrero, Stacy Hall, Lauren Harris, Jacqueline Hubert, Manju Joy, Leela Kuriakose, Phuc Le, Maria Lopez, Hilda Rofheart, Jeane Rummel, Michael Smith, Vivek Srinivas, Diane Travers, Vienna Vivares, Artis Walpool, Jian Zhu, and most of all, Thuc Nguyen. With admiration, I would also like to acknowledge the special expertise of the staff, including Martha Aschenbrenner, Karen Baumgartner, Alejandro Chaoul, Luke Coulson, Deanna Cuello, Macklyn Ivy, Tony Leachman, Natalie Schuren, Katja Sullivan, Steve Thorney, Catherine Tilley, Maureen Valenza, and Carmella Wygant. While all of the physicians are experts in their medical specialty, they approach their work with a gentleness and grace that are remarkable to witness. I would like to thank Joseph Arthur, Shalini Dalal, Maxine De La Cruz, Marvin Delgado, Rony Dev, Daniel Epner, David Hui,

Akhila Reddy, Suresh Reddy, Kim Tanco, Marieberta Vidal, Paul Walker, Sriram Yennu, and Donna Zhukovsky for their openness to my presence on the ward. Nothing would be possible without the exceptional leadership of Eduardo Bruera, the F. T. McGraw Chair in the Treatment of Cancer and Medical Director of the Supportive Care Center at M. D. Anderson. This book is dedicated to Dr. Bruera and to all the members of his team.

Just as the subjects of this book conjoin medicine and the arts, I am extremely grateful to my academic colleagues for their generous readings and thoughtful comments. I would like to thank Nate Carlin, Tom Cole, Leo Costello, April DeConick, James Faubion, Jennifer Fisher, Anne Klein, Sunil Kothari, Jeffrey Kripal, Michael Leja, Alex Nemerov, Elitza Ranova, and Craig Richards. Insightful comments have also been provided by my students Jose Chapa, Sally Huang, Ian Jacobster, Sarah Long, and Andrew Miller. At Rice, expert technical and administrative assistance has kindly been given by Lucinda Cannady, Sylvia Louie, Minerva Romero, and especially, Andrew Taylor. Special thanks also go to Art and Architecture Librarian Jet Prendeville, and to Amanda Focke, Assistant Head of Special Collections at the Fondren Library. I am particularly grateful to Michael Olivas, the William B. Bates Distinguished Chair of Law at the University of Houston Law Center, for providing expert collegial advice and counsel.

Throughout the writing of this book, Lyn Smallwood has been an ideal creative collaborator. Her tender and lovely illustrations have intrinsically shaped and enriched the quality of this text. I am also grateful to Fred Moody for initially introducing me to Lyn, and for his continued interest in my work. At the press, it has been wonderful to partner with the editorial team at John Hunt Publishing. I would particularly like to thank Krystina Kellingley and Maria Moloney for their many valuable insights and for their unfailing kindness and support. Dominic James has skillfully guided this book through production process, and Nick Welch and Stuart Davies have designed a beautiful text. They all have my thanks.

Good friends are a gift, and I am grateful for the special warmth, care, and knowledge of end of life issues shared by my friends Dr. Karen Cottingham and N. J. Pierce. The continued friendship of Rhonda Glick and Sandi Seltzer Bryant have meant so much to me, as have the special friendship, insights, and grace of Pat McKenna. I would like to thank my parents, Joan and Alfred Gagliardi, and my aunt Theresa Glownia, for their support of my work. Since the very beginning, my husband Scott Brennan has been the first person to see me after the day's work at the hospital is finished, and his love, insights, and humor are my foundation.

Above all, I would like to thank the patients and caregivers whose stories are told here. Their wisdom and light fill this volume.

Figure 1. Reproduction of Plate Six in W. Harry Rylands, ed., *Ars Moriendi*, circa 1450; London: Wyman & Sons, 1881, Courtesy Woodson Research Center, Fondren Library, Rice University

Figure 2. Reproduction of Plate Eleven in W. Harry Rylands, ed.,
Ars Moriendi, circa 1450; London: Wyman & Sons, 1881, Courtesy
Woodson Research Center, Fondren Library, Rice University

Introduction

How To Build a Barn: Rethinking the *Ars Moriendi*

The end of life is almost never pretty, but it can be almost overwhelmingly beautiful.

One afternoon I worked with an older woman who spoke only Spanish. Her teenage granddaughter was at her bedside, ready to serve as a translator. This woman was very weak, so I just smiled and asked if I could hold her hand for a moment. The woman took my right hand in her left, and in Spanish she said that my hand felt so fresh. A great sense of peace passed through us, and the woman closed her eyes and fell asleep. As her granddaughter witnessed this exchange, I invited her to take her grandmother's other hand so that the three of us formed a circle around the bed. The counselor who had accompanied me into the room that day later commented that this experience was so valuable because, among other things, it taught the young woman what it means to provide a presence.

This encounter had a magical quality, in part because of the peace that flowed through us all, and in part because of the atmosphere that filled the room. From the moment I stepped through the doorway I noticed not only the two women, but an enormous glass vase perched on a windowsill that held two dozen long stemmed roses in every color imaginable. The sweet scent of the rose petals permeated everything. As we sat together silently, I could see and feel how, in this lovely space, every element had joined together to "provide a presence."

Providing a Presence: An Artist In Residence

Since March of 2009, it has been my privilege to serve as an Artist In Residence in the Department of Palliative Care and

Rehabilitation Medicine at the University of Texas M. D. Anderson Cancer Center. In my "day job," I am Professor of Art History and Religious Studies at Rice University in Houston, Texas, where my research areas include modern and contemporary art history and museum studies, comparative mysticism, and the medical humanities. Despite the notable differences between my research fields, each of these areas shares a common set of themes and challenges, namely: How do we find language to describe states of being for which there is no language? How do we represent the unrepresentable and translate the untranslatable? How do we formulate metaphors of transience to describe subjects that are simultaneously coming into form and going out of form, sometimes within the framework of a single image? And how do we represent the fragile zones of contingency that mark both gradual transitions as well as more dramatic shifts between states of being? Notably, these issues are as pertinent to theoretical discussions of abstract painting's simultaneously dissolving and crystallizing structures as they are to the contemplation of spiritual experience and mystical ecstasy, as they are to the very real challenges of people at the end of life. Thus, throughout all of my work I am fascinated — and profoundly moved — by subjects and situations that repeatedly exceed our capacity to represent them, even as we repeatedly attempt to do so, often through imagery that conveys transitional states and transformational visions.

At M. D. Anderson, my work is sponsored by COLLAGE: The Art for Cancer Network, a non-profit organization conceived and founded by Dr. Jennifer Wheler. Working on both the Acute Palliative Care Inpatient Unit and on the Palliative Care Outpatient Clinic, I assist patients and their caregivers in constructing meaningful narratives to express their insights and experiences. As an Artist In Residence, I serve not as a visual artist, but as a creative writer. While the other artists who participate in COLLAGE's programming variously work in water-

9

colors, Chinese brush painting, sculpture, textiles, and video montage, my creative practice is literary. In turn, the illustrations that appear in *The Heart of the Hereafter* were commissioned specifically for this project from the West Coast visual artist, Lyn Smallwood. While each of the drawings is unique, their soft and gentle qualities display a sense of stylistic coherence. Their appearance is open and general enough to be evocative, yet sufficiently descriptive to convey the details of the individual scenes. Thus the illustrations' delicate features are razor thin, yet just thick enough to hold everything to present a vision of the visions.

Because my primary materials are words, I work in the creative media of language and human consciousness. As the patients and I produce poetic narratives together, my role can perhaps best be described as that of a scribe and a curator of thought, as I ask questions and record the responses they inspire. Thus I primarily serve as a translator, yet much of what I translate is ineffable. I create a context, and provide critical skills, so that people facing extraordinarily difficult life situations have an opportunity for personal and symbolic expression, which then becomes clothed in aesthetic form.

Each situation is unique, and you never know what you will find on the other side of a patient's closed door. As an Artist In Residence, I constantly confront the challenge of creating human connections across a formidable gulf of separation. Frequently, when I initially approach a patient I am told that the work "sounds interesting, but I have no artistic ability." This invites me to respond, "Well, let's just say for a moment that you *did* have artistic ability. What images would you want to write about?" Depending on the circumstances I might also ask, "Where are you from?" or "What do you love to do?" or even more simply (yet never simply), "What do you love?" If the person mentions their family, I will ask them to name their family members and then, working our way down the list, I will say to them, "Can you tell me something wonderful about your husband? About your daughter?" etc. When we reach the very end, I will turn to the person and say, "Now I'll ask you the hardest question of all: Can you please tell me something wonderful about yourself?" While people may find this question challenging, it often provides the crucial thematic element that ties the story together while expressing an insight that other family members cherish.

Sometimes if a person is particularly weak or short of breath, I will just ask them directly, "If you had an image in your mind of something that holds special meaning for you—and it can be anything at all—what would that be?" Very often a flash of illumination will become visible on the person's face, and they will share an image with me. They will describe a subject or a scene, while I gently encourage them to talk and make notes to help crystallize their thoughts. Once the artwork is complete, I read the person's words back to them, while making any additions or corrections that they indicate. The text is then inscribed into a handmade paper journal, which the person is able to keep and share with their family, either as a medium for further creative expression or as a legacy gift that performs a memorial function. The portable microenvironment of the text thus provides a durable yet tender memory of this transient moment in their lives.

Open to the Open

When things are working well, the visits can become quite intimate. As the person and I talk together, they will often imaginatively see, hear, touch, and experience the various loves in their lives. This occurs twice: first, when the person initially tells me their story; and second, and more intensely, when their story is read aloud and they hear the intrinsic beauty of their own words reflected back to them on the surface of the artwork. As we walk gently through this terrain, my status temporarily changes and I go from being an outsider to a momentary insider as we pause together inside the sheltered warmth of the moment.

Yet beyond this brief initial description, there is not an established protocol or predetermined procedure for our interactions. Instead, I have found that the opposite approach works best, as this creative practice requires a significant degree of self-overcoming. People come from all over the world, as well as from half a mile down the road, seeking treatment at M. D. Anderson. Not only are each person and each situation unique, but at the end of life dramatic physical and emotional changes can occur almost immediately. Thus I have found that it is necessary to exercise subtle discernment and to practice the art of allowance while stepping lightly, speaking softly, and meeting everyone's gaze directly so as to see the person and not the illness. In turn, this experience has reaffirmed for me the great value of uncertainty, of not asking for or insisting on anything, while maintaining an open mind, an open gaze, and an open heart. In these tender circumstances, the key is to place no predetermined limits on an unlimited reality. In my own mind, I think of this practice as remaining *open to the open*. By remaining open to whatever arises, it is easy to welcome whatever comes forth.

Not surprisingly, I receive a wide variety of responses to this offering. While many people are open, curious, and enthusiastic, not everyone is equally receptive to the idea of producing an artwork together. Sometimes people are physically exhausted after having returned from a medical procedure or treatment, while others can be emotionally drained after having spent much of the day interacting with a succession of care providers. Others still are drowsy and simply need to rest after having received pain medication. Occasionally, people are intimidated by the idea of working with an artist. And some individuals are emotionally unresponsive because they are living in various states of anger, shock, sadness, grief, or opposition after having received some "very bad news." Sometimes people are either unable or unwilling to confront the gravity of their situation, so they place themselves at a distance from their immediate surroundings and erect a variety of barriers in an attempt to mitigate pain and reduce emotional distress. This can be particularly evident when people are still newly adjusting to difficult news; in these delicate circumstances, a person's emotional withdrawal can be greatly amplified if they are surrounded by overwrought caregivers, or by the overwhelming presence of grieving family members or friends filling the room.

One day I met a middle-aged woman who was the mother of five young children, including a baby who was a little more than a year old. The nurses had informed me that this woman was experiencing "emotional turmoil," and they hoped that I could alleviate some of her anxiety through creative expression. Yet when I asked this woman if I could work with her, and perhaps make something for the children, she immediately recognized the potential emotional impact of the encounter and she categorically refused. With a flat affect and tone of voice, she said, "I'm familiar with your services, and I'm not interested. I'm just not in that place." Notably, such points of resistance can emanate not only from the patients themselves, but from overwhelmed and wary caregivers who assume the role of protective gatekeeper for the person.

In my several years of doing this work, only once has the production of an artwork resulted in a distressing outcome. This situation was particularly complex because the woman appeared to be cheerful and even somewhat robust, and prior to entering the room I was unaware of her unresolved family issues. When I asked this woman about her special image, she smiled and immediately replied, "That's easy—it's my granddaughter." I asked her to tell me about the little girl, and she related wonderful stories that expressed the child's creative and loving character as she described the games they played together. This woman's imagery was beautiful, and when I read her moving words aloud she burst into tears. She then told me that hearing the artwork actually made her feel worse because it sounded like she was going to die, and she wasn't yet ready to die. I stood quietly by the woman's bedside for several minutes while she cried uncontrollably. After leaving the room, I told the counselor about the situation so that she could follow up appropriately. This difficult experience taught me that, on rare occasions, producing an artwork may be too painful for people who have not yet accepted their own deaths, who are in unacknowledged or unresolved states of turmoil and anger, and who are grieving for their lives. While this reaction has only occurred once, I vividly recall the scene and my heart still goes out to this woman.

As this suggests, there is no single, normative response to this work. Just as the artworks generate a striking diversity of expressions, whatever the person's reaction to my offering, the wishes and autonomy of the individual are always respected. Yet for people at the end of life, the stakes of being able to engage positively with the world are extremely high. As the medical researcher Anna-Leila Williams has observed,

> For individuals who have achieved spiritual well-being, the end of life can be recognized as an active, beautiful time of accelerated growth requiring courage, passion, and grace and offering the opportunity to be transformed. However, for those for whom the existential questions remain unanswered, the end of life can reverberate discordantly with despair and anguish.[1]

Thus a broad spectrum of communication is all part of the diverse landscape of acute palliative care. Sometimes people do not wish to produce an artwork together, but to engage in the art of conversation. In these cases, what is most needed is sensitive attention to whatever arises, including acknowledgement of what is not working. Sometimes this involves the art of listening well, and all that needs to be said is, "I'm sorry that you're feeling badly. Thank you for sharing this with me." There are other occasions when people want a sense of human contact that unfolds beyond language. In these cases, the most appropriate thing I can say is, "May I just hold your hand?" Much like the woman whose room was filled with the scent of rose petals, some of my deepest experiences in acute palliative care have occurred at the level of joined hands, closed eyes, and silent connection.

When people do talk, they often tell stories about their home and family, or about perfect moments they experienced in beautiful locations, or about their religious beliefs and spiritual experiences. Because this work takes place in Houston, Texas (and thus, in the Southwestern United States), Christian themes tend to recur in the end of life narratives.[2] However, the production of the artworks could extend to any faith tradition, even as the works do not have to include a spiritual or religious component at all.[3] As this suggests, this aspect of my work as an Artist In Residence resonates with that of a nondenominational hospital chaplain who may encounter a Christian patient in one room, and in the next an atheist, a Jew, a Native American, a Muslim, a Buddhist, or a member of any other faith tradition. Not only is Houston a diverse multicultural city, but people come from all around the world seeking treatment at this renowned hospital. Thus my artistic work implicitly bears the traces of a mini-cultural ethnography that is at once regional and international in orientation. The work requires me to move between numerous perspectives in a single day while producing artworks that are sometimes expressed in explicitly religious language, and sometimes not—yet all of which require me to remain *open to the open*.

While in *The Heart of the Hereafter* I have selected ten love stories—from well over a thousand that I have gathered through the years—that feature vivid descriptions of people's supernatural encounters and transcendent spiritual experiences, only approximately one in four of the artworks engages overtly spiritual or religious subjects. My scholarly book *Words Beyond Words: Finding Language at the End of Life* will feature a broader selection of the themes that arise within this creative practice.[4] Yet with this thematic diversity the issues become, not simpler, but only more complex. In particular, at the end of life the boundary between the domains of the sacred and the profane can be extremely fragile, if not highly porous. Just as the artworks often express these multivalent associations, they raise fascinating questions such as the following: At the end of life, how do we determine what is *not* a spiritual image? Is there anything that arises in this context that potentially *isn't* sacred?

Why we have no Ars Moriendi in our Contemporary World

In previous eras, people at the end of life could consult a spiritual guidebook, an *ars moriendi*, or guide to the art of dying. These small printed books circulated widely throughout early modern Europe, and they represented an extremely popular genre of writing. Featuring a progressive series of illustrations (Figures 1 and 2), the *ars moriendi* taught people how to prepare for death.[5] The plates showed the various pains and sufferings that a dying person faced, and the corresponding spiritual support that they received from the heavenly realm. The illustrations were accompanied by commentaries and prayers to be said while awaiting death, including pleas for forgiveness and entreaties for mediation and intercession so that the soul would be received into heaven. If the dying person were unable to say the prayers for themselves, then others around them were supposed to recite the prayers on their behalf.[6]

In the woodblock illustrations of the *ars moriendi*, the viewer is positioned in a liminal space, as though poised on the threshold of the death chamber and witnessing the scene from the doorway. From this perspective, the dying man's room appears to be "enjambed at the threshold of two intersecting spiritual realms,"[7] and thus situated between the competing forces of darkness and light. Indeed, the dying man's room appears as a meeting ground of the natural and supernatural worlds, a convergent space that is filled with attendant appeals to evil and goodness. Hideous demons taunt the dying person, imploring them to "kill thyself" and end suffering, to succumb to guilt and despair for the sins committed in earthly life, to feel undue pride, and to experience greed for life itself and all of its sensual pleasures. To counter these formidable temptations, arrays of saints, angels, and other holy figures offer comfort while promoting the virtues of faith and humility, patience and endurance, forgiveness and hope.

An illustration from a mid-fifteenth-century *ars moriendi* (Figure 1) shows a dying man receiving such spiritual consolation from saints and an angel after demons urged him to kick out violently against his caregivers in all of the frustrations of his suffering. Counseling the man to show patience, an angel with outstretched wings points upward toward the heavens, while the dying man's own hands are clasped together in a similar gesture of prayer. On the opposite side of the bed, the figures of God the Father and Christ the Son are accompanied by ranks of saints, while defeated demons fall to the floor and hide under the bed.

Just as this image of struggle appears at the midpoint of the volume, the final plate (Figure 2) depicts the moment of death itself. Assisted by a monk, the dying man holds a lighted candle as his eyes finally close. The man's soul, which resembles a newborn baby, emerges from the top of his head, where it is received by a host of rejoicing angels. Appearing at the foot of the bed and triumphing over the defeated demons clustered densely on the ground below is the figure of the crucified Christ attended by saints and apostles. Throughout the volume, saints appear as powerful beings who are at once human and divine, while angels serve as messengers of purity and grace. As this suggests, the *ars moriendi* offered both vivid depictions of, and practical and spiritual responses to, the dangers that the dying were thought to encounter. As such, the book appears like a staging ground in an ongoing battle between heaven and hell—a war for the human soul that turns on the choices made by one person at a time. Ultimately, the *ars moriendi* tells a triumphant story of recognition, illumination, and deliverance.

While the *ars moriendi* was extremely influential historically, no comparable tradition exists today. Our diverse secular society is characterized by a lack of shared spiritual beliefs, and this existential element is largely responsible for producing the situation we now encounter at the end of life. At the same time, this lack of religious closure requires the adoption of a broader viewpoint that engages multiple perspectives simultaneously. Such multiplicity itself represents a very powerful form of letting go.

Given both the practical challenges of the modern healthcare environment, and the philosophical difficulties associated with offering universalizing—and potentially coercive—narratives regarding a "good death," it is appropriate that we currently have no uniform guide to the end of life. While a comprehensive discussion of these complex subjects lies beyond the scope of this volume, I will briefly note that the extensive literature on the end of life offers an array of valuable, if sometimes conflicting, perspectives on these issues. Scholars of religion have discussed the role that sacred rituals and objects can play in preparing people to face death and reach a state of acceptance, while providing comfort and reassurance to mourners during the grieving process. Thus the scholar of comparative religion Gary L. Ebersole has noted the complementary ways in which human experiences and creative representations can inform one another at the end of life. As Ebersole has observed, "The imagining of death is not an empty exercise; it shapes the individual and communal experience of death and life."[8]

Writers in disciplines ranging broadly from bioethics to anthropology and cultural studies have critiqued various aspects of the *ars moriendi* and noted the limitations and risks associated with presenting a uniform script for dying or a universalizing vision of what constitutes a "good death" in pluralistic postmodern societies.[9] And just as there is no unified cultural or theological narrative on death and dying, these activities now often take place in a modern hospital or related healthcare facility, institutional environments that are fraught with their own complexities. Regarding these subjects, the surgeon and writer Atul Gawande has observed that "Dying used to be accompanied by a prescribed set of customs. Guides to the *ars moriendi*, the art of dying, were extraordinarily popular; a 1415 medieval Latin text was reprinted in more than a hundred editions across Europe." However, in our modern age of technologically mediated biomedicine, it is no longer certain who the dying even are. As Gawande incisively points out, "In the past few decades, medical science has rendered obsolete centuries of experience, tradition, and language about our mortality, and created a new difficulty for mankind: how to die."[10] Thus it is not surprising that calls for a new *ars moriendi* have repeatedly cropped up in popular writings. Just as rapid technological advancements continually impact—and in some cases, have altogether replaced—the traditional roles of healthcare providers, it is easy to envision a corresponding need for a customized personal approach to the compassionate care of human lives, up to and including at the end of life.[11]

Applied Aesthetics: Something to Read, Something to Do, Something to Hold Onto, and Something to Let Go Of

As this suggests, there is a clear and pressing need for a discourse that dignifies the death experience and brings it into life, something that we have too often lost sight of. In this volume, I am not offering a universalizing metanarrative regarding what might constitute a good death in contemporary culture. At the same time, my combined experiences as a scholar of the humanities and a practicing Artist In Residence in palliative care have provided a unique perspective from which to view these complex subjects. From this distinct vantage point, the issues appear in a different light. *Perhaps above all, my experiences have repeatedly shown me that the end of life is all about life itself and the many different types of love that we experience as human beings.* Thus rather than adhering to a formulaic, predetermined script such as the *ars moriendi*, my combined scholarly, clinical, and artistic practices have reaffirmed the value of remaining open to whatever arises at the bedside, which is itself a highly liminal, individual, and emergent space. By remaining open to the open, I can be present, so that I can step out of the way, so that the artworks can emerge, so that they can reappear in the book that you are now reading. Just as the stories contained in this volume are ultimately not about death but about life itself, *The Heart of the Hereafter* appears far less like an *ars moriendi* than like an *ars vivendi*, a book on the art of life.[12] And just as there can be no uniform script such as the *ars moriendi* because there is no one way to die, so too do the stories in this volume show that there is no one way to live. Instead, there are multiple ways to be alive, up to and including at the end of life.

When engaging these themes, I think of such an interwoven creative and clinical practice as a form of applied aesthetics. Notably, in its own way the *ars moriendi* can also be seen as an early example of applied aesthetics. At a time when personal agency was so very limited, the *ars moriendi* provided people with something to read if they could read and something to look at if they could not, as well as something to do, and something to hold onto. The *ars moriendi* also presented a vivid sense of connection between multiple realms of being, and thus, a tool for imagining sacred presences amidst extreme states of human suffering. The enduring appeal of such a project may well reflect people's longstanding needs, hopes, and desires to feel a sense of accompaniment when facing the transition between worlds. As the historian David Morgan has commented regarding the power of such religious imagery: "The cultural work that popular images perform is often a mediating one, serving to bolster one world against another, to police the boundaries of the familiar, or to suture the gaps that appear as the fabric of the world wears thin."[13] The traditional *ars moriendi* represents a particularly powerful example of such popular devotional imagery, as it conjoins the sacred and the secular spheres to perform a practical function at the end of life, while also mediating between worlds and establishing order at a time when the world seems to be breaking apart.

In contrast to the imagery of the *ars moriendi*, the artworks featured in *The Heart of the Hereafter* represent not the fixed boundaries between worlds, but the complex relations and openings between them. The artworks display pivotal points of intersection and convergence between various spheres of being and the forms of love expressed within them. Thus both in comparison and in contrast to the *ars moriendi*, the work of the contemporary Artist In Residence may well represent a type of rite of passage, but it is one that is fashioned gently on the spot, in the moment, in the open spirit of the encounter.[14]

In turn, the narratives that appear in this volume were all produced in, and implicitly reflect, a compassionate healthcare environment that can accommodate and honor such visions. *The Heart of the Hereafter* can thus be approached as a form of applied aesthetics that offers something to see and something to read, just as the stories potentially provide something to identify with, something to envision, something to hold onto, and something to let go of—or better still, something to let go with. Yet rather than being a guide to teach people how to die, the love stories are offered to help people to live.

Through compelling first-person accounts of extraordinary personal and spiritual experiences, each chapter vividly expresses the love that transformed people's lives. The stories are distinctive, yet each one represents a source of extreme wisdom, insight, and grace. And therein lies the value of the artworks, not only for the dying, but for all of us who are living here right now. The stories can change not only how we view the end of life, but of how we view life itself, and thus how we actively live our lives when we encounter the part of ourselves that is nothing but love.

And so many different types of love, at that. More than we could possibly have imagined.

And Go With Love

One day on the ward I met a middle-aged woman who shared several tender images of her family, some of which centered on the hardships they had all endured together, and some of which focused on cherished traditions and memories of the holidays. This woman concluded her artwork with some brief yet powerful words that are as meaningful to the living as they are to those at the end of life. As if addressing everyone all at once, this woman said to

Step forward
And go with love.

Given the nature of these subjects, this book will likely elicit a variety of responses from readers, ranging from skepticism to belief, from sadness and fear to laughter and joy. For individuals who gravitate toward rationalist frameworks and who may not have a bank of personal spiritual experience to draw on, the stories may seem overly idealistic. And for those who approach the issues of terminal illness and the end of life with great fear and sadness, the stories may seem too optimistic, and even overwhelming. For these reasons, I encourage readers to remain open to the possibility of being open. This book will provide an unexpected perspective on the types of extraordinary experiences that can—*and do*—arise at the end of life. None of us can know in advance the impact that such knowledge can have, either now or in the future, either for ourselves or for those around us. Thus I encourage everyone to approach the stories in a spirit of openness. And while this is a small book, please do not hurry through the reading. Take your time. As you read, your heart will show you which stories resonate for you. Each of the artworks contains an almost incandescent paradox, namely: In witnessing another, to what extent are we also witnessing our own hearts, yet in a new light? Again and again the stories show us that, what seems impossible, is possible. By engaging these themes, the artworks can be seen not only as texts and images, but as complex states of consciousness that can evoke powerful feelings as they take us to the limits of language itself while palpably expressing what it can mean to be present to one another. And just as the stories offer multiple perspectives on love, life, and spirituality, the text is written for everybody.

How To Build a Barn

When people go to build a barn, one board holds another board, which then holds another board. In this book I present ten detailed situations, each of which expresses a particular type of love, and one layer builds on the next. The stories go into the grains of the wood and they lean on one another, opening up pathways of learning and expansion through the different types of love that flow through the volume. Beginning from the ground up, the foundation of the text lies in philanthropy, in the collective love that guides the communal actions and outreach activities that human beings undertake on behalf of one another. The framework of the text then builds outward from individual self-respect to romantic love and familial belonging, before turning to the various aspects of spiritual love that are expressed through grace, forgiveness, enlightenment, and exaltation. While the different types of love are presented in differentiated terms, the various loves overlap with one another as they recur throughout the book. And just as the scenes range broadly from the domestic and the familiar to the ineffable and the transcendent, a sense of discovery repeatedly comes from knowing the secret that love is the piece that carries both the heavy and the light sense of grace, and the strong sense of gratitude. At the end, the structure of the text folds back on itself, both practically and philosophically. Ultimately philosophy appears as a kind of doubling, as the love of wisdom becomes reflected in the wisdom of love.

Figure 3. Lyn Smallwood, *Learning is Freedom, It Comes from the Heart*, 2013, graphite on Arches paper, 12 x 9 in.

Chapter I

Philanthropy: Learning is Freedom, It Comes from the Heart

One afternoon I was working on the Palliative Care Outpatient Clinic where I met a quiet, middle-aged couple. The wife was the patient, and she sat inside a treatment room waiting for the doctor and his team, while her husband ventured out into the lounge to get a cup of coffee. From a short distance away, the man saw me working with another patient and he became interested in the Artist In Residence service. When I had finished the artwork, the man approached me, introduced himself, and brought me inside the corner treatment room to visit with his wife.

Immediately I noticed that this attractive, brown-haired woman was wrapped up tightly in a green thermal hospital blanket as she sat in her chair beside the treatment table. Her pale hands were clenched in pain, and every few minutes she twitched with little spasms that seemed to exhaust her. I smiled gently and asked the woman where she and her husband were from. We began to talk casually about a range of subjects, as the woman described the details of her home and her professional career. For several decades she had served as a special education teacher in the local public school system. While her students ranged in age from kindergarten through adulthood, most of her work took place at the elementary level. I told her that I too was a teacher, and that I cherished my time in the classroom. Warming to the subject, the woman proudly informed me that "teaching is my biggest purpose in life." Speaking with great conviction, it was clear that education was not only her profession, but her calling. As she shared various details of her classroom experiences, the woman's eyes lit up and her body gradually began to relax. The tremors of pain eased considerably as she became peacefully absorbed in her topic.

The woman observed that

Teachers equate the ability to read with IQ. I still remember the first student I ever had. He was in elementary school, and his mother had just dropped him off. One of the first things he ever said to me was, 'The tutors all think I'm stupid.' After I worked with him for about a month, this boy was standing up on the school bus route and reading all the road signs out loud. The other kids on the bus clapped and gave him a standing ovation. This first student of mine would go on to finish college. The first time many of these children ever read was in my class.

This woman's special skill and passion lay in empowering children who had been marginalized and dismissed by others, and she put her whole heart into her teaching. While the local school district only allotted a limited number of hours of individual instruction per child per week, this woman voluntarily put in extra time after school to work one on one with the children. As the students' language skills improved, they became more visible, both to themselves and to others around them. The positive influence that this woman exerted had long-lasting effects, as she made learning accessible in ways that continued throughout the students' academic lives. Her artwork is entitled,

Learning is Freedom, It Comes from the Heart

Teaching is my biggest purpose in life,
And I taught for many years.
My students were the kids who had always been told
That they were the ones who couldn't learn.
In the children's minds, they always thought of themselves as

"stupid."

They had labeled themselves as being not as smart as the others.

The most wonderful thing was,
Once they started reading,
They couldn't get enough.
They were like a sponge.
This made me feel good,
Because I could always see the difference in the students,
And how proud they were.
That's how I'd like to be remembered,
As doing for others.

Learning is freedom,
The freedom to go anywhere and do what everyone else does.
These kids went beyond anything they ever dreamed of.
They loved the freedom that learning gave them.
Learning is freedom.
It comes from the heart.

As I read these powerful words aloud, both the woman and her husband were moved to tears. After a few minutes they had composed themselves, and the man told me that there was more to the story. The woman then briefly described her own very difficult childhood, and the inspiration and strength she received from a divine source:

If I were to order my life, God would be in charge.
God is the source that everything comes from.

I was born into difficult circumstances,
And I was determined to lift myself up.
As a little girl, an angel came and told me that
Life would not always be this way,

And that everything would be alright.

I have always loved angels.
I have quite a collection of angels,
All different kinds.
And I know that there are angels here on earth,
Guiding us.

Reflecting these themes, Lyn Smallwood's graphite drawing (Figure 3) appears to be both radiant and grounded.[15] The scene is at once light and serious as a teacher stands in front of a blackboard before a crowded classroom, where rows of students are seen from behind, seated at their desks. On various levels, this is a scene of doubling. The long blackboard that holds the day's lesson appears to be faintly haloed in white light, as if to underscore the idea that learning is a kind of illumination. In a gesture that is both practical and metaphorical, the children raise their hands to answer the teacher's question, yet they also appear to be reaching upward toward the sky. As this scene unfolds on the ground below, a gentle yet powerful angel in a flowing white robe is poised above the center of the blackboard. With outstretched wings and arms, this glowing figure watches over the work that takes place in the classroom below, perhaps guiding the lesson. In turn, the teacher's facial features bear a subtle resemblance to those of the angel who stands in front of a shimmering dark background that recalls the surface of the blackboard. In both the upper and lower registers of the composition, the teacher and the angel appear as intermediaries, as presences who support the growth of others while serving as links between worlds.

Just as the details of the artwork are very specific and concrete, they engage larger themes concerning the relationship between personal strength and collective empowerment. In this woman's classroom everyone mattered, and no one was ever overlooked or forgotten. Through her teaching the woman was able to restore a sense of hope, clarity, and support to those who were struggling, while helping them to feel valuable and worthy. Just as she taught her students how to read, this woman was like a mirror that showed them their own intelligence as she taught the children to believe in themselves.

In yet another mirroring, the woman's story also reflects the ways in which her perspective was transformed both through the hardships that she had suffered as a child, and by the reassurance that she received from an angel. This early spiritual encounter provided not only an immediate source of comfort, but the lasting strength that enabled her to undertake such challenging life work. The angel appeared as a kind of heavenly role model who, early in life, taught this woman what it meant to have faith in another and to express that faith through love. Now at the end of her own life, the memory of the angel evoked the presence of grace and a sense of divine accompaniment during another particularly difficult juncture of her life.

This woman's story is at once ordinary and extraordinary, modest and powerful, as her artwork reflects a life of service to the local community just as it opens up to the heavenly realm. Viewed in broader terms, this love story engages not only one woman's passion for teaching and dedication to her students, but larger themes of compassion, ethics, and philanthropy. The *Oxford English Dictionary* defines philanthropy as the "love of mankind; the disposition or active effort to promote the happiness and well-being of others; practical benevolence, now especially as expressed by the generous donation of money to good causes."[16] Just as gifts of "money to good causes" are often associated with charity rather than with philanthropy, one of my own students commented insightfully on the distinction he perceived between the two types of love:

I see charity as giving to a cause, and I see philanthropy as *being* a cause...I like that the *OED* describes philanthropy as *'practical* benevolence' because there is necessarily a practical component...[with philanthropy the] love of mankind is so strong that, at both the internal and external levels, the philanthropist *has* to do something to help others.[17]

Viewed in this light, philanthropy represents the power of love in action, in which the gift of a person's contribution offers a tangible form of "practical benevolence."

Grounded and elevated at once, philanthropic work recognizes the uniqueness and the value of another as well as what we all share in common as human beings. In this woman's narrative, there is no conflict between subjective affirmation and surrender, of being in service to oneself, the community, a professional calling, and a higher spiritual power. Rather, this story both encompasses and transcends such dualities. Seen in this light, "the classroom" is at once a practical and a metaphorical space of transformation, a place for restoring pride and dignity to those who have been deemed less worthy, and for openly recognizing the value of others and instilling in them a strong sense of well-being and self-respect, or *amour propre* (a theme that is discussed from another perspective in the following chapter). Now at the end of her own life, the recognition of these accomplishments brought this woman deep joy and pride.

I have intentionally opened *The Heart of the Hereafter* with a story that powerfully demonstrates that "learning is freedom, it comes from the heart." On various levels, this complex artwork reflects the interwoven practices of making visible and being seen. Perhaps most concretely, the teacher helped to strengthen and make visible children who were otherwise invisible by using language skills to empower their presences. On a more subtle level, the artwork also reflects the value of teaching and learning about seeing the unseen, of making the invisible visible. Like all of the artworks that appear in this volume, this opening story offers a powerful image that helps us to recognize the invisible within the visible, and vice versa, as we enter into an illuminated space, an epiphanic moment in which the poetic, the existential, and the visionary domains all converge. And in this way, the pictures that appear in *The Heart of the Hereafter* can be seen as teachers that "help us to learn how to read."

In a complementary sense, writing about the end of life poses the related challenge of how to make the often invisible presences of the dying visible in contemporary culture. In one sense, we are all like the children who benefitted from the expertise of the teacher who showed her students their own value as she taught them "how to read." When we enter into the deep terrain of the end of life, we often encounter a realm where such learning and the wisdom that it engenders are truly boundless. Seen in this light, the love stories are powerful teachers of the intertwined processes of creation and recognition. As such, the stories bring light to light.

Figure 4. Lyn Smallwood, *Red Like the Heart, and Autumn Gold*, 2012, graphite on Arches paper, 11 x 8 ½ in.

Chapter 2

Amour Propre: "I Am a Warrior": Red Like the Heart, and Autumn Gold

Before I entered this man's room, the medical staff had cautioned me that there were some strong emotional and communication difficulties associated with this particular individual. Actually, whenever I hear the words "strong emotional and communication difficulties," or "particularly difficult patient," (and yes, even "borderline hypoactive delirium"), I tend to get excited because I know that there is genuine potential for an extraordinary visit. Each time I enter a patient's room, I remain open to whatever arises, and sometimes this involves listening closely and acknowledging what is not working well. Sometimes nothing comes forth at all, while other visits have proven to be extremely powerful. This was one of those occasions.

Although he was very weak and drowsy, this middle-aged man was eager to work together, to produce an artwork that would make his complex spiritual imagery concrete both to himself and to those around him. Perhaps most striking of all was that, despite the extreme pain and disfigurement of his advanced metastatic cancer, this man continued to see and describe himself as a warrior. As he proudly told me, "That's my spirit. That's my way."

Throughout our visit, this man drifted between various states of consciousness. As I sat at his bedside, he closed his eyes and described scenes of his actual experiences hunting game in the woods of his northern home. These descriptions were interspersed with images of himself as a warrior hunting and tracking big game in the autumn woods, accompanied by Native American spirit guides. Now anticipating his own death, this man traveled freely between these alternating realms of thought.[18] He said that, when he hunted last autumn, he knew in his heart that this would be his last hunt. As he told me, "It felt inside like 'I'm done hunting.' There's still venison in our freezer from last year's hunt." He then spoke in detail about his garden at home. I asked him if particular plants were important to him, and he mentioned squash and other vegetables that provided food for the family table. As we spoke, it was clear that this man was poised between the familiar world of life experience and a visionary mode of consciousness. Bridging the two domains were images of the animals he saw in the woods while hunting, and which he now saw again in his mind's eye. He described the deer, the rabbits, the salmon, the ducks, and the geese, and he said that "all of the animals are going home now, to their homes in the woods." We held hands throughout the visit, and this man cried while I wrote his words. After we completed the artwork, he was tired and needed to rest, and I asked him if he wanted to let go of my hand. He said no, that he rested while holding my hand.

This man's end of life story vividly interweaves the various faiths with which he identified, including Native American and Roman Catholic traditions. Despite their differences, this man told me that he was in the process of reconciling these perspectives because "Now I see them all as one way of knowing." He also perceived sacred presences throughout the natural world. In his artwork these expressive themes became manifested chromatically, as well. When I asked the man which colors he wanted me to use to write his personal narrative in, he looked me straight in the eye and replied, "Red like the heart, and autumn gold." His story strikes all of these chords simultaneously:

Red Like the Heart, and Autumn Gold

I am a warrior.
It's in my heart.
I'm a big game hunter.

I hunt deer in the woods by my home.
That's my spirit.
That's my way.

I also gather food and grow vegetables.
There's Thanksgiving, and the family table.
That's what it's all about.

I'm hunting now.
I'm with Sitting Bull and the Warriors.
I'm also Roman Catholic,
And I can put them all together now.
They're all connected.
Now I see them all as one way of knowing.

I'm not afraid of death, and it's upon me.
I'm at peace with myself.
We all hunt and track together as one.
It's in my heart.
I am a warrior.

When I read these words aloud, the man thumped his chest very hard and proclaimed that *this* was what was in his heart. With tears in his eyes, he told me that he wanted the artwork to be featured at his memorial ceremony.

Reflecting the man's story, Lyn Smallwood's pencil drawing (Figure 4) connects multiple layers of personal and archetypal imagery to create a scene that is at once vividly concrete and deeply metaphorical and metaphysical. In this illustration the forest becomes a world of symbols and forms, shadows and reflections. Throughout the surface of the drawing, alternating patterns of darks and lights create a strong sense of design, while contrasting elements provide the primary structuring forms of the composition. Following the interior pathway of the image, the strong vertical lines of the tree trunks cast long diagonal shadows along the forest floor. The tall trees frame the composition, while creating a sense of interior depth that extends into the distance and culminates in a clearing that is filled with light. Along this pathway, a few stark tree limbs and stray rays of light connect the two sides of the drawing, just as they crisscross the circular entrance of the aperture. A Native American figure walks along the forest path, while a short distance away, a deer pauses at the opening and turns to face him. Both the hunter and the deer appear to be solid yet etheric as they stand poised at the edge of the rising light.

Expanding on this warrior imagery, the man told me, "When hunters hunt, they make their kills quickly. I'm not afraid of death, and it's upon me. But I do fear the pain of the illness and the dying process." Thus in this difficult context, warrior imagery provided this man with an archetypal framework to describe who he was, how he lived, and how he wished to die. He was adamant that he did not want to undergo the protracted illness, weakness, and suffering associated with advanced cancer. Instead, he wanted to die quickly and naturally, as much like a warrior as possible.

All of which made him "a particularly difficult patient" from the standpoint of institutional biomedicine. This man had recently begun to receive a new type of technologically advanced radiation therapy that required him to enter a device where he was physically immobilized for the duration of the procedure. He had already received one such treatment, and the experience generated so much anxiety and distress that the session had to be discontinued. While this new therapy could potentially have extended his life by several months, it would have been necessary for him to undergo additional rounds of treatment, and he absolutely did not want to do this. Instead, he wanted to die quickly, and he asked the medical team to facilitate his passing.

Initially, some of the healthcare providers saw this man's response as his "refusing therapy and wanting to die." This situation created a great deal of distress both for the medical team and for the patient and his family, some of whom saw his choice as a form of prematurely giving up. Even after my visit, some people dismissed the artistic imagery as a type of escapism, and one healthcare provider commented that they found it odd that this man preferred such hunting imagery to the real world. Yet others quickly recognized that the man was making a larger statement concerning his priorities regarding quality of life, and they realized that the warrior imagery provided valuable insight into his perspective, as well as a common vocabulary for discussing what was vividly real and important to him. In very practical terms, there was now concrete imagery that opened up a new avenue of communication regarding quality of life issues and the range of options that were available. Ultimately, the entire team played an important role in this man's care, and he was able to return home to spend the last month of his life in his house by the woods. Shortly after leaving the hospital, the family sent a photo of the man sitting in his beloved garden, admiring his plants, and smiling.

This story represents a vivid example of the role that the Artist In Residence can play in contributing a complementary perspective to the work of the interdisciplinary palliative care team.[19] Because this complex case presented so many different issues associated with optimizing the quality of life for an initially resistant patient, and because it involved the combined efforts of the entire team, the case was presented several times to audiences at the Texas Medical Center.[20] After one such presentation, a very senior palliative care physician made an extremely generous comment. He remarked that, in all of his years of providing patient care, he has found that he can write a prescription to alleviate pain, but that he can't write a similar prescription to relieve suffering. This presentation showed him how the work of the Artist In Residence can help to address human suffering, which in turn can help to ease pain.

Notably, Dame Cecily Saunders, the founder of the modern hospice movement who pioneered the treatment of pain for dying patients, identified crucial connections between human suffering and the various types of pain that people encounter at the end of life. They include not only the physical pain of the body, but the social pain of financial and cultural crises, the emotional pain associated with feelings of helplessness and isolation, and the spiritual pain that arises from the need to feel safety and find meaning in life. Each of these factors represents a dimension of what Saunders termed "total pain." As she observed, "It isn't enough to treat the physical pain alone, although this is important. The whole person is suffering, so the whole person must be treated" so that care "can reach the most hidden places."[21] In turn, just as all caregivers inevitably work with their own conceptions of their roles, this story illustrates some of the ways in which the Artist In Residence program can help to address various dimensions of pain — particularly those that involve the relations between physical and non-physical pain that can emanate from a variety of psychosocial, existential, familial, psychological, or spiritual sources — while contributing to a larger team effort dedicated to the alleviation of suffering.

This story represents a vivid example of the power of aesthetics to provide a common meeting ground by making concrete representations of the extraordinary — and often highly elusive — states of consciousness and spiritual insight that can, and do, arise at the end of life. By expressing these inner states outwardly, the artworks can help to facilitate communication and promote a sense of mutual understanding between the person and the world around them. Without such a tangible mode of expression, these inner visions might otherwise remain invisible. This point is especially important because, at the end of life, people sometimes experience altered visions of the self and the world. Such states of consciousness can crystallize in composite spaces that I think of as "worlds between worlds." In these intricate, shimmering zones, the familiar surfaces of the existential world become embedded in the symbolic, and vice versa.

This was the case with the man who saw himself as a warrior hunting in the woods with his spirit guides. Such imagery provided a means of expressing the insight that death is part of the natural cycle of life. And this, too, is a love story. *Red Like the Heart, and Autumn Gold* expresses the man's love of nature and the earth, the love of life itself, and his love of the mystical presences who accompanied him. Yet perhaps above all, this story represents a singular expression of *amour propre*—of self-love, self-esteem, and self-respect. While this man's choices were initially perceived as a form of prematurely giving up and turning away from others, his story appears in a different light when viewed through the lens of *amour propre. Amour propre* can be seen as a foundational element that creates the possibility of forming loving bonds between the self, the world, and those around us. As such, it is the love that "makes all other loves possible."[22] *Amour propre* teaches the vital lesson that a person must be present to themselves before they can be present to another. This man's sense of *amour propre* was further complicated by a fundamental paradox, as his choice to live authentically in his own presence required others to accept the shadow of his impending absence.

In such extremely challenging circumstances, preserving the integrity of personal identity amidst the fragmentation of terminal illness itself represents a type of heroism. The warrior image provided this man with a powerful model of fighting for his right to live and die with dignity, just as it united his image of himself with that of divine presence. This story brought the man back to himself and created a template for his being in a state of integrity at the end of his life as the courage of the heart, *le coeur*, became vividly expressed in shades of red and autumn gold.

Figure 5. Lyn Smallwood, *The Navy Uniforms*, 2013, graphite on Arches paper, 11 ¼ x 9 1/8 in.

Chapter 3

Agape: For the Love and Respect of the Service: The Navy Uniforms

"Would you please go in and work with this man? He has no family anywhere in the area, and he's sitting all alone in his room, writing."

By the time this visit occurred, I knew very well that the nurse's brief description could mean just about anything. As always, I approached the man's room while remaining open to the open. I knocked gently on the door, introduced myself, and asked if I could visit with him for a few moments. All of which is to say that I walked into this man's room with absolutely no expectations. Yet within a short while, an intricate story was emerging. I asked the man where he was from, and to our mutual surprise, we discovered that we had much in common. This man originally came from New York, although he had left the northeast in the late nineteen fifties (I was born nearby, in Connecticut, in the mid-nineteen sixties). We also found that we shared the same mixed ethnic heritage on both sides of our families. Now we sat together, so many decades later and thousands of miles away, in his hospital room at M. D. Anderson.

This man and I quickly made a strong personal connection through our mutual knowledge of, and deep affection for, the far-away world of a mid-century, Italian-American home. We shared an understanding of its beliefs, customs, and values. As we talked, this other world felt so far away and yet so very real and near, and it lay at the heart of the story. This man's artwork centered on the male relatives of his family and their strong connection to the Navy, a tradition that extended from his grandfather to his father, his uncles, himself, and his son. This older man was also a war veteran who was very tough and grounded in his perspective. So it was all the more surprising when he shared a story of supernatural appearances. This man told me that, when he was a young man, his deceased grandfather and father came to him at a critical juncture in his life. Now the memory of their presences was returning to him at the end of his life, another crucial moment of transition. His story is entitled,

For the Love and Respect of the Service: The Navy Uniforms

For my image,
I go to my son and my family.
I include all of them,
Because we have stayed together through all the problems
And not gone our separate ways.

First, I need to tell you that the name James is sort of sacred in our
*   family.*
My grandfather was James, Senior.
His son, my uncle, was James, Junior.
And I'm Robert James.

The best thing I can say about my family
Is that there is one night I've never forgotten.
Once a week, the whole family showed up at my grandmother's
*   house*
To have a meal together.
We ate in the dining room, and we were a large family.
But the two chairs at the head of the table
That were my grandfather's chair and my father's chair
Were always left empty after they passed away.

That night, I was just getting ready to sit down and eat
When one of my uncles turned to another uncle and said, in a loud
*   voice,*

"What are we going to do about this boy?"
I had just joined the Navy earlier that week,
But I hadn't told anyone yet.
As soon as my uncle said those words
I looked up from my chair and I saw my Granddad in his Navy
* uniform,*
And I saw my Dad in his Navy uniform.
They both had been dead for years,
But they were sitting there at the table in their Navy uniforms.
And then I saw my two uncles, who were in street clothes,
Wearing their Navy uniforms.

I knew I had to join the service
Because of the love and respect I had for these men,
And the love and respect they had for the service.
And I knew that, if I didn't join the service,
I could never sit down with them at that table again.

After I read these tender and powerful words aloud, this man and I held hands for a few minutes. He was very grateful for the visit, and he particularly appreciated the handmade journal, because he said that he had some more experiences he wanted to record.

Lyn Smallwood's illustration (Figure 5) is set in an Italian-American home in New York during the late nineteen fifties. Delicately rendered in graphite on Arches paper, the drawing's atmosphere is soft and intimate as an extended family sits down together at a long, formal dining room table. Much like in traditional homes of this era, two wooden colonnades flank the outer edges of the high-ceilinged dining room, while in the room beyond, a sideboard holds assorted china. This drawing is presented from the perspective of someone who has just entered the dining room through the open doorway that leads in from the kitchen. The tip of the dining room chandelier glows brightly overhead and provides a source of emphasis and contrast that opens and illuminates the scene. The chandelier also centers the composition visually as it establishes a direct linear pathway that extends through the middle of the long dining room table. This primary sight line ultimately leads to the dark wooden door that frames the grandfather's luminous presence at the head of the table.

In this multi-figure composition, the dining room table appears symbolically like an extended family tree. It's as though one of the man's uncles has just loudly asked, "What are we going to do about this boy?" and gestured down the table toward his nephew, while the entire family looks up and over at him. In turn, the young man himself has also just looked up from his seat at the foot of the table to see his grandfather and father in their Navy uniforms. His grandmother is seated in her customary place at her husband's side. Next to her are the man's two uncles, followed by family members of all ages, ranging from elderly people to very young children. Everyone is dressed formally for Sunday dinner. The two younger uncles wear sailor's white middy shirts, while the grandfather and father are senior presences dressed in the suits of Navy officers, with decorations on their chests. The scene culminates in the bright glow of their Navy uniforms, an etheric vision that stayed with this man for the rest of his life.

Notably, *The Navy Uniforms* contains highly concrete and detailed imagery that combines an intensity of visualization with emotional poignancy and deep spiritual insight. Taken together, these elements create a sense of suspended temporality—a lucid state where time seems to stand still—and this quality is as compelling as it is heart opening. In turn, this man's narrative engages many different states of being. The story begins with the immediate physical context of an older man sitting alone in his hospital room at the end of life. Our visit together opens up a youthful memory of the time when he first joined the Navy, and his grandfather and father appeared to him in spirit form. On so many levels, this type of reminiscence conjoins various states of love and longing, presence and absence, being and nonbeing— while drawing them together in a unified realm. This complex domain forms the imaginative space of the artwork.

Often during the production of an artwork, a person will begin in one state of mind and body, and they will experience additional states of being as the visit unfolds. When the artwork is complete, the person returns to their physical surroundings in a slightly altered form, one that is more uplifted. These transitions can help to renew the spirit and perspective of the person at the end of life. As we work together, I have often witnessed people enter into a deep state of peace, to unclench their hands, to uncurl their bodies from a fetal position, and to stop trembling. It's as though the person's subtle bodily memories and experiences help to strengthen and transform their physical condition and bring them to a more elevated place inside of themselves.

At the same time, these uplifted states are often associated with narratives that are very concrete and sensual. Much like this man's story of his grandmother's dining room table, end of life narratives can be extremely visual, aural, and tactile, just as they can engage a strong sense of taste and smell. Deep bodily memory is both sensitive and etheric, and it seems to inhabit a state of consciousness that is parallel to the time and place in which the person is actually living.[23] In this way, this creative practice engages fascinating questions concerning the relationship between embodiment, art, and time. The artworks repeatedly demonstrate the power of embracing the intensity of an actual lived moment, and then watching the limits of that moment become transcended in an aesthetic space where the moment arises anew again. Artistic activity is often poised delicately between various registers of consciousness, and creating an artwork together can provide an imaginative opening that closes the space between them.

Along these lines, I have also frequently observed that, at the end of life, a person's surroundings can become extremely constrained, as the world appears to shrink before their eyes. Yet in these very limited circumstances, seemingly little things can become monumental. As a different perspective emerges, so too does an altered sense of scale and proportion, and in this state bodily memories and experiences are not constrained by familiar parameters of time and space. Such intricate convergences of multiple states of being take us far beyond familiar models of Cartesian mind/body dualism. Paradoxically, at the end of life there can be an expansiveness of vision that recognizes the large within the small, the numinous within the ordinary, and the past and the future contained within the fullness of the present. These qualities are further heightened when the stories are illuminated by the power of love.

The Navy Uniforms tells such a complex, ambivalent story that evokes both the lights and the shadows of familial connections, as expressed through the sense of duty that the man felt in continuing the family legacy in the military, and the corresponding sense of shame that would have ensued if he did not follow in his father's and his grandfather's footsteps. These tensions arose before his eyes once again in a scene that culminated in the sight of his father and grandfather appearing in spirit form, a vision that filled this man with a sense of wonder, love, and belonging.

Reflecting these themes, his artwork expresses a deep love and affection for the home and the family, and the men's collective love and respect for one another and for the military service. This story honors multiple generations of a family while acknowledging the connections that united them. Such love is characterized as agape, and it is selfless and caring. Notably, agape also connotes a type of love that is associated with a ritual communal meal, a feast that carries sacred overtones.[24] In many traditional Italian-American homes of this era, both food and family were seen as sacred. On that particular evening in New York in the late nineteen fifties, the dinner was especially sacred for a young man whose grandfather and father appeared to him in spirit form to acknowledge his contribution and his place within a larger scheme of being. This vision joined multiple generations of a family, just as it crossed the boundaries of life and death to let this man know that he was not alone.

By engaging these themes, *The Navy Uniforms* presents a different perspective on a phenomenon that scholars refer to as "social death."[25] While some people at the end of life are surrounded by caregivers, others are alone and thus far more isolated. Just as a person's physical body dies, so too can their sense of identity correspondingly become diminished. These processes can occur as part of a person's drawing inward and disengaging from the world at the end of life, or from family members withdrawing either physically or emotionally, even regarding the person as if they had already passed on. Thus while the individual is still alive existentially, it is as though they have died socially.

As this suggests, at the end of life there is often a strong need for connection in the wake of potential alienation. Some people find reassurance through caregivers who continue to assert their sense of belonging. Other people turn to religion and spirituality to affirm links to a world beyond. And still others express a connection to family members who have passed on, thereby seeking a sense of continuity that transcends the familiar parameters of time and space as well as the boundaries of life and death itself.

This chapter began with a nurse asking me to work with a patient at the end of life who had no family in the area, and who

49

sat all alone in his room, writing. Throughout our visit, it was clear that this man drew on a communal bond that gave him comfort and strength, just as his mystical artwork reflected his sense of accompaniment by the unseen presences of the grand-father and father who, so many decades ago, showed him a vision of life continuing after life.

Figure 6. Lyn Smallwood, *The Other Side of the Waterfall*, 2012, graphite on Arches paper, 6 ¾ x 8 ¾ in.

Chapter 4

Eros: What it Means To Be Truly in Love: The Other Side of the Waterfall

One day I worked with the wife of a man who was very near the end of his life.[26] The couple had traveled a long distance to receive care at M. D. Anderson. Before I entered the room, the medical staff informed me that, due to the progression of this man's advanced intestinal cancer, he could no longer speak. Yet his devoted wife was by his side and she very much appreciated the company. The social worker also told me that "it is a true love story with this man and his wife." A moment later I knocked on the door, and I immediately saw the accuracy of this description. When doing such sensitive work, you develop the ability to read the atmosphere of a room almost instantaneously. This particular room was filled with love, and I knew that it would be a pleasure spending time with this couple.

Before I could ask where they were from, the woman started talking. She told me that her husband is of Native American heritage, and that they had been married for nearly a decade. While he had lain in a semi-nonresponsive state for several days now, I could sense this man's tremendous presence of spirit and his great love for his wife.

We visited together for well over an hour, and the woman was frequently in tears as she recalled the story of their meeting and their courtship. She also described the unique home that they had built together high up in the mountains. These themes blended to form the artwork, the centerpiece of which was a striking image of

The Other Side of the Waterfall

The first time I met my husband
I would look at him,
And his face would change.
I saw three different faces during that first hour.
I knew I had made my match.

With my husband, it was always an adventure,
Because I never knew where he was going to take us next.
We would take camping trips,
And I saw how much he loved the water.

Most of the time we'd come home to the mountains.
We have spectacular views.
We look out at the edge of the haze,
And we look at the rising sun.

Once we went high up in the mountains
And we were sitting together
On the other side of a waterfall.
As we sat there looking out at the falling water
I knew that this was what I always wanted.

And then I knew what it meant to be truly in love.

Like all of the narratives that appear in this volume, this is a true story. Throughout our visit, the man had remained unconscious. Yet when I asked the woman, "Can I read you the story that I just heard you tell?" her husband stirred in his bed. He briefly woke up, and he even sat up and swung his legs over the side of the bed. The man became conscious and started smiling at his wife. While he did not speak, he indicated with a gesture that he very much wanted to hear the story. Sitting together on the bed, the man and woman held hands and looked at one another so tenderly while they heard the story.

The original narrative was considerably longer than the fragment that appears here, and as I read the woman's words aloud, the couple smiled at one another as they recognized the small details of their life together. After I finished reading the story, the woman said that I had captured it, and she thanked me. Almost immediately afterward, the man had to lie down again and, a few minutes later, he was nearly nonresponsive. It was as though the man had traveled back through the other side of the waterfall—that he briefly came through the curtain that separates realms of life and states of consciousness—in order to be present with his wife once again and sit with her, for just a few moments, on the other side of life itself.

Lyn Smallwood's graphite drawing (Figure 6) presents a striking image of contrasts and joinings. Perched up high on a sloping mountainside, a couple sits together on the edge of a boulder, while streams of cascading water flow past them. The textured surface qualities of the drawing are created through pencil strokes that alternate between being lightly intermittent and densely packed, just as the overall scene emerges through these linear contrasts and conjunctions. In this image the man and woman also sit together as two, even as their clustered forms blend together as one as they watch the falling water. Flowing rapidly down the mountainside, the currents of the waterfall are extremely powerful, just as they remain abstract and elusive. The inner crevice of the mountain forms a protected space from which to observe this dramatic meeting of earth and water. This space is at once solid and void, craggy and smooth, just as it is filled with darkness and light, action and stillness. Similarly, in the extended narrative the couple's home high up in the mountains placed them on firm ground, just as it gave them an elevated perspective with "spectacular views" of the ways in which the haze could melt the solid surfaces of rock when seen through beams of rising sunlight.

By engaging these themes, this story represents a striking example of eros, a form of romantic love that is expressed on the physical, emotional, and spiritual levels. Eros is a love of conjunction and complexity, as an individual is seeking outside of themselves at the same time that they are cultivating inside of themselves. Such love passes through the inner and the outer realms while weaving a single world between them. Much like the man's tender gesture of taking his wife's hand while listening to their story, the philosopher Jean-Luc Nancy has similarly observed that the lovers' caress represents "the being of the other being in me," just as it marks a state of uniqueness *and* of joining as two become one by remaining two.[27] This intricate joining of two as one was the intimate form of love that I saw before my eyes, in the hospital room at M. D. Anderson.

In his classic study of *The Four Loves* (1960), the scholar and author C. S. Lewis offers a compelling definition of eros as "that state which we call 'being in love'; or, if you prefer, that kind of love which lovers are 'in.'"[28] Lewis observes that eros floods every part of a person, just as it "obliterate[s] the distinction between giving and receiving." Given these qualities, Lewis characterizes eros as a state of love that is filled with immersion and reciprocity. From a very different perspective, that of historical psychoanalysis, another classic account of eros can be found in the writings of Sigmund Freud. While Freud's psycho-analytic discussion differs decidedly from Lewis's Christian narrative, Freud also draws on images of fluidity, melting, and melding to characterize eros as an exceptional state of human self-overcoming. As Freud observed in *Civilization and its Discontents* (1930), "At the height of being in love the boundary between ego and object threatens to melt away. Against all the evidence of his senses, a man who is in love declares that 'I' and 'you' are one, and is prepared to behave as if it were a fact."[29] Thus despite their significant differences, both Lewis's and Freud's highly influential formulations of eros engage metaphors of fluidity to describe the union of two as one.

As I sit with people at the hospital and ask about their cherished images, again and again they speak of their precious connection to, and deep and continuing love of, the person with whom they have shared their life. In this context, C. S. Lewis is prescient when he notes the ambivalence of eros, so that "even when the circumstances of the two lovers are so tragic that no bystander could keep back his tears, they themselves—in want, in hospital wards, on visitors' days in jail—will sometimes be surprised by a merriment which strikes the onlooker (but not them) as unbearably pathetic." Indeed, amidst their tears people will often smile and laugh together—and even, at one another— at the end of life. The grandeur *and* the lightness of eros can be almost overwhelming. Just as the love stories that emerge during such visits are always deeply personal, they also contain a quality that both touches and transcends the lives of the two people involved, as the love seems to continue with a life all its own.

Reflecting these themes, the image of being on *The Other Side of the Waterfall* evokes a timeless quality that further illuminates and intensifies eros. If I were to phrase the relationship between time and timelessness in technical terms, I would say that *The Other Side of the Waterfall* demonstrates how eros can become a locus of suspended temporality when placed within an aesthetic framework.[30] That is, just as lived experience flows like water, the artwork delicately crystalizes the scene into solid form so that we can consciously recognize what we are seeing, feeling, hearing, and knowing. And in this way, the work of art can become a work of love.

Finally (but never finally), *The Other Side of the Waterfall* not only presents an intimate image of eros, but it also serves as an intriguing metaphor for end of life experience itself. While viewing the scene from "the other side of the waterfall," it is possible to see life itself from the opposite perspective than is customary, which is the reverse view of the world that typically appears before our eyes. "The other side of the waterfall" can serve as both a concrete existential image *and* as an evocative metaphor for visualizing a space between worlds. Much like the cascading streams of water, such extraordinary experience is elusive and evanescent. Like love itself, it is something that you can reach out and touch and almost hold onto. Almost, but not quite.

At the end of life, this man took his wife to the other side of the waterfall so that they could tenderly recall their love and hold hands just one more time, for just a moment.

Figure 7. Lyn Smallwood, *Haloed All Around*, 2012, graphite on Arches paper, 12 ½ x 7 ½ in.

Chapter 5

Storge: I Knew Then That My Mother Was With Me: Haloed All Around

While I couldn't see what they were all laughing at, I could tell that it was something really funny. A middle-aged woman sat propped up in bed, surrounded on either side by her two sisters. The family resemblance between the women was particularly striking as they all clustered together in front of a small laptop screen that was perched on the patient's tray table. I knocked on the open doorframe and introduced myself. When the woman in the bed heard the word "artist," she brightly called out, "Come in!" and gestured for me to come around to the head of the bed so that I too could see the image that brought these women so much laughter. One of the sisters obligingly stepped back so that I could squeeze in and view the computer screen. Evidently one of the women had a new baby grandson, and they were all laughing together at a charming photograph of the infant wearing his first Halloween costume. The baby was dressed up as a little pirate. Particularly adorable was the contrast between the menacing outfit, complete with miniature skull and cross-bones, and the tiny angelic face that looked out with round blue eyes and long eyelashes. Before long, I was laughing right along with them.

We ended up having a lengthy, moving visit. This woman's special image was based on an experience that she had had more than three decades ago, yet which she still recalled vividly. The subject of her story was at once natural and supernatural:

Haloed All Around

I have one image.

This only happened to me one time,
And it's never happened again.

When I was a young bride,
My husband had to travel a lot for work.
One time my husband had to go out of town,
And I was left alone with our son.
He was only a few months old at the time.
I was at the layette table changing his diaper.
I looked over my left shoulder,
And I saw a woman in a bright blue dress.
She was haloed all around.
I knew it was either my mother or my grandmother.
I waited a minute,
And I turned around,
And she was gone.
It was very brief,
But it made me feel very warm all over.

Then one time
I had a chance to be alone with my father and talk with him.
I was sitting with him in the kitchen
And we were having a drink together.
I said, "Dad, I know you don't believe in these things,
And I don't believe in them either..."
And then I told him the story.
He said, "Your mother was buried in a blue dress."
I hadn't known that, but it felt good to hear.

My own mother died very early.
I was only a young child at the time,
And I wasn't allowed to go to the funeral.

There's a lot of togetherness in our family.

My mother was a wonderful person.
She wanted me to know that
She was there with me,
And that she knew I had my baby.

As this woman told her story, I could palpably feel a sense of love coming into the hospital room. Just as the woman shared a love story that connected various generations of her family, including those who are here and those who are not, it felt like their mother's presence was with us in the room, standing beside her daughter once again.

In Lyn Smallwood's illustration (Figure 7) a young mother stands at a layette table, smiling gently while changing her infant. An older woman in a dark dress appears by her side. The pointed corners of the square window frame and the upright platform of the wooden layette table contrast sharply with the tender, rounded forms that fill the scene. A family resemblance is evident in the women's facial features. This sense of kindredness is further heightened by the visionary quality of the soft pencil drawing. Through the use of reverse shadowing, the artist employs the white sheet of the paper to create a delicate aura around the figures. The scene is set in a darkened room that is illuminated by diffuse early morning light filtering in through a window along the left edge of the composition. Dressed informally in a long white bathrobe, the young mother seems to be glowing in the dawn light. The older woman standing by her side is enveloped in a field of white light that makes her appear to be "haloed all around" as she smiles softly and looks over with great pride at her daughter and her baby grandson.

Through the intergenerational maternal connections that thread through this story, *Haloed All Around* presents a type of love that is known as storge. Storge is associated with the natural affection of parents, especially mothers, and their children. As C. S. Lewis points out, storge is the earliest form of love that we experience, and it epitomizes the sense of warmth and comfort that comes from being together. Such love poignantly encompasses the home and the family, and it is the oldest love that we know.[31]

Haloed All Around combines the groundedness of such domestic warmth with a transformational element of mystical spirituality. The artwork reflects the ways in which a private, ordinary scene can become infused with extraordinary experience, just as a familiar presence came to this woman in such a remarkable way to show her that she was not alone. This encounter brought the woman a feeling of warmth and a sense of maternal love that helped to sustain her with her own child. This memory stayed with her throughout her entire life, along with the knowledge of how deeply she was loved.

Viewed symbolically, *Haloed All Around* exemplifies the ways in which light can be seen as connecting various realms of existence. Like many of the artworks that appear in this volume, this story seems to glow. It is as though the words themselves have haloes, miniature threads of light that conjoin realms that are often seen as disparate from our own, while making visible worlds that we might not see otherwise. Much like *The Navy Uniforms*, *Haloed All Around* shows how such intergenerational connections can unite a family and foster a greater sense of community, particularly at important, transitional moments in a person's life. The powerful effects of this experience extended to the very end of this woman's life. Again and again, when producing the artworks, we go into old garments to find the golden threads that connect life and the afterlife through living links of love.

Figure 8. Lyn Smallwood, *In the Palm of God's Hands*, 2013, graphite on Arches paper, 10 ¼ x 8 in.

Chapter 6

Grace: In the Palm of God's Hands

The young girl sat propped up in a wheelchair, lovingly attended by her father. Immediately I noticed that the girl's face and body were pencil thin, while her limbs were swollen with severe lymphedema. And then I saw her beautiful smile and the special light that filled her soft brown eyes. Initially, I thought that the father and daughter were leaving the Palliative Care Outpatient Clinic, because the girl's wheelchair was facing the door that I had only just walked in through. With a twinge of regret, I assumed that I had just missed them. But then they turned around and entered the waiting area while a prescription was being filled. I went in and introduced myself as an Artist In Residence, and we all started chatting. The young girl told me that she also writes, but that the subject has to be very focused in order for her to get started. I offered her a handmade paper journal, which she accepted gratefully. As we discussed how she might begin the journal, a delicate and powerful narrative emerged as the girl told me a love story about parents and children. The leitmotif of the story was her daily prayer of peace and grace:

In the Palm of God's Hands

Every day I pray.
I just think about God all day,
And His holding me in His hands.

I'm in the palm of God's hands.
That's the safest place to be.
It puts me at ease.

To think about that makes me feel wonderful,
And very peaceful.

I go there every night
When I say my prayers.
I get to this place
And I just sit there
In the palm of God's hands.

Going through something like this,
You act like a child.
I want to be a kid right now.
They don't have a worry in the world.
My parents deal with me,
And they love me.

I think about them holding me.
They have me in the palm of their hands.
Like God,
In the palm of His hands.

This young woman only had a few weeks left to live. On that day, she was very thoughtful as she told me how her mind kept returning to that one lucid image. I inscribed her words on the first page of the journal. I also asked her whether, if she hadn't had this experience, she would still have this same image in her mind. She said yes, she thought she would. I then asked her what she would like to hold in the palm of her own hands. She replied,

I just have thoughts of wellness. I don't see myself like this forever. I see myself in good health, with stability, and with kindness. I only wish I could hold my health in the palm of my hands and command it to do my will. But I can't. Now, it's not a question of asking 'Why?' but of saying, 'It's all in Your hands.' That's what I do in my prayers. I take it one day at a time. And I see God standing there, holding out His hands. But you have to ask God for this, because He's not going to give it to you unless you ask. As long as it's in His will, there is nothing that God cannot give you.

Lyn Smallwood's image (Figure 8) depicts a child curled up in utter peace *In the Palm of God's Hands*. Playing on expandable degrees of scale, it is as though the hands of divine presence can become whatever proportion is most suited to hold whatever rests within them. In this image, the two hands appear to be suspended in time and space as they gently cradle a sleeping child. The pencil drawing displays a fluid circular composition that is both open and closed, suggesting the warmth and solidity of touch as well as the impalpable quality of light. While the drawing's dark outlines are crisply delineated to show the child resting so securely in the palms of the hands, the image becomes progressively lighter and more abstract along the outer edges, as the wrists and arms ultimately disappear off the white sheet of the page and into nothingness. This image evokes the magnitude of a presence that extends far beyond what the eye can see, while tenderly enclosing the fragile life that it holds so gently before us.

In this narrative the young woman's love of her devoted family — storge — appears as an analogue to her experience of heavenly love and being held in a state of grace. Through such human and divine parallels, the young girl saw herself as a child surrounded by her parents, while she was also held by a heavenly presence who comforted and sustained her in peace and love. Such vivid imagery evokes the quality of a theophany. According to the *Oxford English Dictionary*, a theophany is "a manifestation or appearance of God or a god to man."[32] Through the gift of the theophanic image, an otherwise unseen divine presence became visible to this young woman as a source of comfort and love. Such theophanic experiences often contain the quality of a revelation—in this instance, one that became expressed through the fragment of a human form, an image that provided a source of infinite love and grace.

Sometimes when I visit people at the end of life, I get the sense that they are inhabiting multiple worlds at once. It is as if they are simultaneously experiencing multiple states of being. When I enter a room, I can tell right away if a person is in this state because their physical appearance changes and they become extremely beautiful. Make no mistake—there is absolutely nothing pretty about this scene. The person is at the end of life from terminal cancer, and they have suffered greatly, both from this deadly disease and from the effects of the harsh treatments they have received. Yet it is precisely *because* the circumstances are so extreme that the contrasts are so striking. When a person has entered a state of grace their tone of voice changes and becomes soft and kind, yet also extremely confident and self-assured. Even if the person is very weak and frail, their overall appearance shows a heightened state of conscious awareness. Yet perhaps most striking of all are the person's eyes, which glow with a light that is at once deep and soft, gentle and brilliant. This light illuminates everyone in the room and everything in their presence. Whenever I enter such a room I feel deeply humble, and I give thanks with all my heart for the privilege of being present with a person who has entered a state of grace.

Grace is a multilayered construct whose meanings extend broadly from the practical to the theological. The expansiveness of grace is as beautiful as it is striking. The *Oxford English Dictionary* notes that grace (*grātia, grātus*) is variously associated with beauty, favor, mercy, gifts, freedom, and gratitude.[33] Among its many meanings, grace signifies elegance, charm, and a fluid ease of movement. Grace is also associated with permission and gratuity, with privilege and dispensation. Grace exemplifies the willingness of a gift that is freely given, particularly one that is made in honor of someone else. In both familiar and theological terms, we often hear the phrase "by the grace of God," which conveys such a sense of mercy, favor, and gratitude. Similarly, "to say grace" is to give thanks and acknowledge all that has been given to us.

From yet another perspective, grace represents a reflection of one's lot in life, or "The share of favour allotted to one by Providence or fortune; one's appointed fate, destiny, or lot; hap, luck, or fortune (good or bad)." This definition also arose during the visit with the young girl when she said that she wished she could hold her health in the palm of her hands and command it to do her will, even as she realized that she could not. What she could do, however, was to describe the vision that brought her such sustained peace and comfort. As the *Oxford English Dictionary* notes, this form of grace relates to "the divine influence which operates in men to regenerate and sanctify, to inspire virtuous impulses, and to impart strength to endure trial and resist temptation" and it is "often spoken of as *the grace of God*" (emphasis in original). For this young woman, the bottom line was what the Christian theologian Paul Tillich called "the ground of all being,"[34] as the girl envisioned the two hands of divine presence joining together to provide the supporting foundational base of her existence, a state of grace that she experienced as being held *In the Palm of God's Hands*.

Notably, the *Oxford English Dictionary* also includes a definition of grace as "the same regarded as a permanent force, having its seat in the soul." This is the meaning that comes to mind whenever I see the distinctive qualities of a person at the end of life who has entered a state of grace. On another day, I encountered a woman who was eager to share her extraordinary spiritual experience. While we only had about ten minutes together before the attendants wheeled her down for a radiation treatment, those few moments were enough for this woman to tell her story. Initially the doctors believed that she had a respiratory infection, but the infection just didn't heal. Further tests revealed advanced cancer. As she sat in the doctor's office and heard the news, this woman found herself living a version of "the peace of God, which passeth all understanding" (Philippians 4.7):

The Peace That Passes All Understanding

A few months ago I learned that I had cancer,
And I didn't have the response you'd expect.
I had the most peaceful feeling,
Like I'd been wrapped in a warm place.
It felt soft and fuzzy,
And I was totally enveloped.
I felt so peaceful.

It's like I knew that,
Whatever happened,
I was being taken care of.
In church I had heard that God's peace passes all understanding,
But at that point, I got the full application of that peace.
It wasn't until you feel that peace
That you really know it.

Just as this woman described the sensation of being wrapped up in a soft, warm place where she was totally cared for, her narrative is distinct from, yet similar to, that of the girl who saw herself being held in the palm of God's hands. Both images are filled with a sense of ease and balance. As grace surrounds a person, they experience the security of being enveloped in warmth and softness. At the same time, grace also provides courage for the person to expand outward, to become more open to the open. Taken together, the gestures of pulling in and reaching out become reciprocal aspects of a single embrace that encloses itself as it opens up to another. When people enter such a state of grace, it's as though a boundary has melted between something that the person has entered into and something that has entered into them. In these extraordinary situations, self-assertion and self-transcendence become simultaneous expressions. Even as they are one, they are more than one. I always know when I am in the presence of such grace because I can see both the softness and the strength—and, amidst all the pain—the unbelievable light.

This was certainly the case with the young girl who expressed such a powerfully convergent vision of affirmation *and* surrender, as she was at once surrounded by the tender love and warmth of her family while also being cradled in an etheric vision of faith that she eloquently described as being held *In the Palm of God's Hands*.

Figure 9. Lyn Smallwood, *For Goodness' Sake*, 2013, graphite on Arches paper, 10 ¼ x 7 ½ in.

Chapter 7

Caritas I: And Then I Knew There Was a God in Heaven: For Goodness' Sake

At no time was it more necessary for me to remain open to the open than the day I visited with an elderly African American man.[35] This visit almost didn't happen at all, and now looking back, *I* thank goodness that it did. Very often when doing this work, timing is everything. When I came onto the ward that day, this man's nurse was assisting another patient, so I never received the initial feedback on this individual. No one on the medical staff mentioned him to me either, so I simply assumed that he was an off-service patient, and I gave first priority to the people whom I knew for certain were on palliative service. As a result, this visit occurred late in the afternoon, at the end of a long day. This older man was all alone in his room and eager to talk.

From the beginning, he generously called the visit a gift, and he opened up almost immediately. He also broke down in tears several times during the visit, sometimes covering his eyes with a napkin, as though he could not bear to look at me, or for me to see him. He told me, "My God has been so good to me, with the gifts and blessings He's given me. The biggest gift is my grand-children, and the love of my parents and grandparents." He also told me about his daughter and how much he loved her and how hard she had worked carrying all the burdens of the family, including burying all of the relatives. The man again covered his eyes with a napkin while he cried and told me his story. He said, "Lady, I won't lie to you. I got out of prison the Thursday before Thanksgiving last year. I came out in a wheelchair." He had been doing fine for a little while, but then a few weeks ago he became "deathly ill." This man had an aggressive form of stage four prostate cancer that had spread throughout his bones. When he complained of back pain in prison, he was shrugged off and told that the pain came from standing on concrete floors for so many years. Since "every prisoner has a complaint," he was ignored until it was too late and treatment was no longer an option, as the cancer had metastasized so widely.

Again, the tears started to flow as he closed his eyes and said, "Lady, I won't lie to you. I've been the murderer, the robber, the rapist, and the thief. I'm guilty of way more than anything they convicted me for. I spent so many calendar years in prison. I had been locked up for about five years, and I found my loving God." He then said that, if this hospital room were hell, there would be one corner where people were doing one set of things, and one corner where they were doing another, and then he pointed to the far corner of the room by the door and he said that he would be in that corner: "I'd rather be among those who are sitting there, trying to pray their way up, than those sitting there, accepting their fate. I'd rather be with those who tried to pray their way out of hell." His story is entitled,

"For Goodness' Sake"

Those were my Grandmother's words,
And she used to say to me,
"Boy, do this for goodness' sake,
For the sake of goodness."
I didn't get the meaning of that until a year ago,
The Thursday before Thanksgiving,
When I got out of prison.

I was locked up for so many calendar years.
When I had been locked up for about five years,
I found my loving God.
In prison, I prayed,

"Please God, let my child forgive me."
Two weeks later,
My daughter came to prison.
She is such a special child.
She stood at the table.
Out of the clear blue sky, she said,
"Daddy, I forgive you.
I forgive you with the full measure
That I want to be forgiven for my sins."
She came back and verbalized the prayer
As I had said it.

And then I knew what it meant to do something
Purely for the sake of goodness,
For goodness' sake.
And then I knew there was
A God in heaven.

Lyn Smallwood's graphite drawing (Figure 9) depicts a man kneeling on a hard concrete floor in a prison cell, with his hands covering his face. In this narrative, the man described himself metaphorically as being in a corner of hell, praying to God. Reflecting this imagery, in the drawing the figure is folded in on himself, just as he is reaching out to the heavens. This stark setting displays an unusual quality as the scene seems to overpower the man, who is bent over in a pose of supplication and humility. The repeating rectilinear patterns of the jail cell contrast with the man's rounded, sloping form. Paradoxically, this vulnerable figure appears to be both diminished and glorified by the scale of his surroundings as he prays in a large open space that seems at once daunting and luminous. The delicate, sketch-like quality of the image heightens these paradoxical effects as it contrasts the solidity of the concrete wall that the man immediately faces with the open lattice grillwork of the cell door. Within this ambivalent space of darkness and confinement, of sorrow and prayer, sunlight pours in like bands of hope, and the solid metal bars of the cell seem to dissolve in their radiance.

As I sat with this man in the hospital room, he cried again when I read his story aloud because he said that his daughter's words were exactly as I had spoken them. This man had spent a great deal of time working with the prison ministry, which provided a Christian framework to express his experiences. Thus the pattern of his narrative is particularly suggestive. When this man initially prayed in prison, his direct appeal to God represented his first request for forgiveness. When his daughter subsequently repeated his words during their visit together, her repetition became a second enunciation, which, in his mind, confirmed that his prayer had been heard and answered. Finally, our visit together allowed this man to see his prayer in a new light. Hearing both his words and his daughter's melded together in a single story line represented a third enunciation, which served as a powerful affirmation, and which may have been part of his liberation.

This man's story is about finding grace and recognizing the meaning of goodness while serving time, while time serves you. That is, while incarcerated this man experienced repentance, sorrow, and the power of "finding God" and receiving forgiveness. During his daughter's visit his prayer came back to him "out of the clear blue sky," and the sky opened up before him. Now, at the very end of the day, an artist unexpectedly came into his room and wove the pieces together while reflecting the story back to him as a single vision. In these extraordinary circumstances, the artist performs something like a witness function, a critical affirmation in which people tell me their stories so that there can be a surfacing to consciousness of something that is often lying just below the conscious level.

People tell me, so that they can tell themselves, through the words and images that surface to the surface at the end of life.

The effects of such stories can be very powerful, as this man was lifted up by the restorative force of his own words. This story demonstrates how artworks can enable a process of recognition through enunciation and representation. Both the words and the tears that flowed from this man created a larger pattern of release and emergence as his descent into emotion preceded an ascent into spirit. As such, the man's story can be seen as an example of the fullness of such an emptying (*kenos*) and its subsequent crystallization into imagery (*eidos*). That day, the streams of the kenotic and the eidetic crossed one another to form the substance of the artwork.

In this tender context, the title of the man's narrative is especially significant. The phrase "for goodness' sake" literally means to do something for the goodness of God. These words initially came from the man's grandmother during his boyhood. Now as an elderly man at the end of his life, these powerful words returned to him as he recalled his encounter with his daughter. In both scenarios, a sense of goodness was expressed through the man's intergenerational connections to the women in his family. His story is filled not only with familial love or storge, but with goodness itself and with the expansive love of divine presence, which is called *caritas*, or charity. Much like the phrase "for goodness' sake," another familiar expression is that "charity begins at home," and this man's love story could not have been closer to home.

The word "charity" carries both Christian and non-Christian associations. According to the *Oxford English Dictionary*, among its many meanings charity signifies "love, kindness, affection ...especially with some notion of generous or spontaneous goodness."[36] When the secular and the theological meanings converge, the concept of charity becomes particularly relevant. Charity connotes a state of "love and right feeling" towards others, just as it is "the Christian love of one's fellow human beings; Christian benignity of disposition expressing itself in Christ-like conduct." These various meanings are evident in both the contrasts and the content of the man's extended narrative. As he candidly told me, he was "the murderer, the robber, the rapist, and the thief. I'm guilty of way more than anything they convicted me for." He had committed multiple violent crimes, including taking someone's life, for which he spent the remainder of his own life in prison, until he encountered the deadly disease that ultimately took his life. This part of the story can be seen as the opposite of love, as expressed through terrible acts of violence, trauma, and destruction. These scenes of violation were part of the suffering that filled this man's vision of hell. When he found God through the prison ministry, he prayed that he might experience love, forgiveness, and redemption. This too relates to the Christian conception of charity as a two-fold love that encompasses man's love of God and God's love of man. The conjunction of the human and the divine realms in *caritas* produces not only a love of God and of one's fellow beings, but a charitable "disposition to judge leniently and hopefully of the character, aims, and destinies of others, to make allowance for their apparent faults and shortcomings." It is for these reasons that C. S. Lewis calls charity a gift that is so powerful that it "enables [a person] to love what is not naturally lovable".[37] Charity extends to everyone equally because such love recognizes the divinity inherent within another person, including "the God hidden in the prisoner whom [one has] visited." As such, charity appears as both a gift and a tool of grace.

Interweaving these associations, this man's story passed through the dark shadows of human nature and experience, and ultimately found affirmation in the love of family, God, and goodness itself. The artwork represented a place where all the paths converged in forgiveness and grace. Notably, just as one aspect of grace involves "mercy, clemency...pardon or forgiveness," to "forgive" is to grant a gift, to release and surrender, to pardon and let go.[38] As seemingly opposite states of being are folded together as one, this story also demonstrates that the subject of heaven on earth can be closely related to its opposite—to the searing pain of hell on earth. I have found that such hell can emerge at the end of life when there is great physical, emotional, or spiritual pain, which can come from an overwhelming sense of fear, anger, guilt, loneliness, suffering, struggle, or lack of acceptance. Clearly, this man was in a place of profound guilt, and he was seeking forgiveness and release through the conscious acknowledgement that his words had been heard and his prayer had been answered.

Two days after our visit, this man passed away peacefully at M. D. Anderson.

Figure 10. Lyn Smallwood, *Our Hearts are the Same*, 2012, charcoal and pastel on white Canson paper, 12 1/8 x 9 in.

Chapter 8

Caritas II: In the Garden with Jesus: Our Hearts are the Same

Everything about this middle-aged woman expressed sweetness. She was a diminutive figure in a pink silk bed jacket, which was elegantly draped over her hospital gown. In a tiny voice, she told me that she had studied music in school, majoring in both piano and vocal performance. She was also an amateur visual artist who painted in oil and watercolor. When I asked her about the types of subjects that she liked to paint, she replied, "Above all, I love flowers. I see things, and I just want to capture them in paint." Her favorite flowers were the huge white stargazer lilies and the large pink and white peonies that grew in the gardens in her family's "mammoth yards." She particularly loved these flowers "because they're so unstaged and natural." She had spent many hours carefully observing the lighting and backlighting that came at different times of day, and she was intrigued by the abstract forms that the flowers assumed with their rich, saturated colors. As she proudly told me, "I painted these flowers for my family, and they were really beautiful, without a doubt."

When I asked this woman if she had a special image in her mind, not surprisingly she immediately described elements of her family's extensive gardens. Yet her narrative also included her pre-death spiritual visions, which were informed by her Christian faith. Above all, this woman described her daily visits with Jesus Christ, as the two sat together, arm in arm, under a cherry tree on a marble bench in her family's garden.[39] Her story is entitled,

Our Hearts are the Same

I have been blessed with so much in my life.
There is an image that I have,
That I go to bed with every night.
And then I'm not afraid of anything.

I'm in a garden, like my family's garden.
There's a huge chokecherry tree
With a large flowering canopy
And underneath the chokecherry tree
Is a beautiful white marble bench
With dappled shade on it.
Here I am on the bench, sitting next to Jesus.

We're just sitting together peacefully on the bench,
Arm in arm.
We're not even thinking of death.
Everything is right with the world.
We understand each other,
And we love each other.
Our hearts are the same.

Later in the visit, the woman elaborated on her spiritual experiences and the ways in which her faith was helping her now:

Five Leaps Toward Jesus

I also have this vision every time I wake up.
If I'm worried,
I immediately change my thoughts
To taking five leaps toward Jesus.
He's just happy to see me,
And to be together.

I know the minute I step off the path
And start worrying, I'm a wreck.
So I just jump back on his trail.
I cannot tell you how that lifts everything worrisome
From me.

At the end of our visit, I asked this woman about the source of her spiritual strength. She spoke frankly about the near-death experiences that had occurred in her family. This woman's mother had almost died in childhood from acute peritonitis. As she lay in her bed in pain, the little girl looked up and saw "an angel perched over the doorway, who looked like a beautiful lady in a pink dress." The child told her mother, who prayed to the angel and to God that God's will be done. The little girl survived and grew up, and one day she told this story to her own daughter, the woman who now lay in the bed at M. D. Anderson at the end of her life. As this woman candidly told me,

> After facing death and seeing the angel, my mother was not afraid of anything, and that gave me strength as I grew up hearing that story. When I received that cancer diagnosis, I was already Stage 3, and the doctor told me it was as if a plane had just landed on me, that I probably only had six weeks left to live. That was several years ago. When I received that diagnosis, the Holy Spirit was already in me to catch the news. My heart didn't miss a beat. Faith is the best anesthetic, and the more you have, the less unnecessary worrying.

Lyn Smallwood's mixed media drawing (Figure 10) fuses natural and supernatural elements. Rendered in soft charcoal and pastel, the image depicts a woman sitting on a marble bench, arm in arm with Jesus, beneath a flowering cherry tree. The tree's curving trunk and exposed limbs form the intricate patterns that structure this floral and spiritual imagery. The cherry tree's exposed branches are topped with clusters of buds and blossoms that create a soft white canopy; this gently rounded form also complements the subtle halo surrounding the figures on the ground below. While the stark, fragile tree limbs suggest the woman's impending death, the emergent blossoms are signs of continuing growth and new life. The use of soft charcoal gives the drawing a tangible material quality, which creates solid yet dissolving forms that evoke the misty atmosphere of the garden. The white pastel that forms the halo appears to be at once chalky and translucent. The halo creates a soft yet palpable presence that joins Jesus and the woman together in a shared circle of light.

Like the story of the young girl who was held *In the Palm of God's Hands*, this woman's image of sitting in a garden with Jesus displays the quality of a theophany. As noted above, a theophany is a visible manifestation of divine presence. In these artworks, the showing of the sacred appears in very human terms. Because this woman's image of sitting in a garden with Jesus came at the end of her life with terminal cancer, the garden imagery implicitly evokes Gethsemane, "the garden outside Jerusalem mentioned in Mark 14 as the scene of the agony and arrest of Jesus." More broadly, the term Gethsemane also connotes "a place or occasion of great mental or spiritual suffering."[40] Yet this woman's image could not have been further from a garden of sorrow or anguish. Instead, she described a garden of tranquility, a beautiful place that recalled the love of her family and her intimate connection with Jesus Christ.

This woman's sense of love and communion with Jesus were reportedly so complete that she felt that *Our Hearts are the Same*. As such, her love story represents an expression of Christian *caritas*, or charity. In the previous chapter, I told the story of the prisoner who experienced *caritas* as the love and forgiveness that came to him *For Goodness' Sake*. While that man found the presence of God while living through a version of hell on earth, this woman's experience of *caritas* was expressed through a vision of heaven on earth. Yet despite their considerable differences, both artworks convey a mutually reflective form of Christian love that encompasses "God's love of man" and "man's love of God" fused together in a state of oneness. Both stories also evoke the broader associations of *caritas* as "love, kindness, affection" and "generous or spontaneous goodness." This woman's experience of *caritas* centered on the mystical image of her sitting with Jesus, a figure whom C. S. Lewis characterizes as a model of "divine life operating under human conditions."[41] In this case, the conditions were so human that the woman felt as though she and Jesus shared a single heart. This sense of love and understanding sustained her so deeply that she was lifted above her pain and fear, and her "heart didn't miss a beat."

These vivid images were in this woman's mind well before I ever entered the room. The artwork merely recorded and crystalized the scenes that were already so present to her. Like the unstaged natural beauty of the flowers that filled her family's garden, this woman's stories of her and her family's near-death and pre-death experiences surpassed the boundaries of language itself, just as they provided a source of enduring strength that shaped how she died and how she lived.

This woman passed away a week and a half after our visit. While I was not physically present at her passing, one of the healthcare providers who attended her at the bedside described the serenity that filled the room. He told me that, just before she slipped into unconsciousness, this woman raised her head, looked all around her, and thanked everyone for her wonderful life.

Figure 11. Lyn Smallwood, *I'm Calling It Enlightenment*, 2013, graphite on Arches paper, 9 5/8 x 9 in.

Chapter 9

Enlightenment: Now, I'm Just a Conduit, So I'm Calling It Enlightenment

In a gentle yet clear voice, this woman emphasized how much she wanted her story to be shared. This was the last thing that she said to me, and she said it twice before I left the room. Like all of the people whose narratives appear in this volume, in the hours that we spent together this woman became my teacher. Now it is a privilege to bring the story full circle and present it here, in the chapter that you are about to read.

As I turned the corner beyond the Nurses' Station, I ran into the attending physician who was in charge of the Palliative Care Inpatient Unit that month. We smiled warmly at one another and exchanged greetings, and then the doctor gestured toward the room immediately to her left and suggested that I go in and work with that particular patient. I ended up spending more than two hours with this fascinating woman. She was an artist and a businesswoman, the former CEO of a company. She was also in the final stages of leukemia, so this was a contact isolation room and I was fully covered in gown, gloves, and mask.

This was another visit that almost didn't happen. The woman had just received some pain medication, and initially she told me that she preferred to rest. She also poignantly remarked that she had finished her last painting and put down her brush, so she wasn't sure exactly what we would do together. Yet she was curious, and she asked me about my work as an Artist In Residence. We began chatting, and the conversation just didn't stop. Our discussion ranged broadly from art and architecture to culture and travel, to comparative religion and various systems of spiritual belief. As we spoke about sacred subjects, the woman told me that, while she did not formally adhere to any religious tradition, she had strong Tibetan Buddhist leanings, and she found this perspective to be particularly valuable and inspiring.

Throughout our visit this woman was absolutely glowing. She described the transition she had recently made from being in a state of excruciating pain to one of relative comfort, which the palliative medications had made possible. Our conversation ultimately became an artwork entitled,

I'm Calling It Enlightenment

For so long, I've been in such intense pain.
The pain was all-encompassing.
Many people were sending me love from all over the world,
And I couldn't receive that love.
Those were the bad days.
Then I came here,
And I just surrendered.
I felt the release of that pain, and the letting go,
And the light of my friends and the unconditional love came
    through.

Before yesterday, I felt a little radiant.
Yesterday I had a breakthrough
And today, I feel completely radiant.

I keep thinking: Is this death?
It's letting go,
And I keep thinking,
If this is,
It is so beautiful.
I don't know what to call it.
It's very difficult to put in words.
And now, I'm just a conduit.

So I'm calling it
Enlightenment.

As I read her powerful words aloud, this woman said that I got it, and then she covered her eyes and cried. For several minutes I held her hand while the tears streamed down her cheeks. Then she became very calm and peaceful, and she asked me if she had died. I told her no, that she was still alive, but that my sense was that she was experiencing multiple states of understanding. She said that she had never been able to express this before, and she couldn't believe that I had captured it. She asked me how I did it, and I told her that she did all of the work and that these were her own words and I was merely the scribe and so, like her, just a conduit. She said that she wanted her story to be shared, and I promised her that I would do my best. Then we hugged, and I stepped away from the bed. When I reached the doorframe the woman asked me to remove my mask, which I did. And then we looked into one another's eyes and really, truly smiled.

When I returned to the hospital the following week, I learned that, three nights after our visit, this woman fell asleep and she didn't wake up. She slipped into a coma, and the following day she passed away peacefully at M. D. Anderson.

Lynn Smallwood's illustration (Figure 11) displays multiple layers of light and shadow to evoke the complex experience that emerges in this woman's narrative. In this scene, one glowing presence arises from another to suggest a being who is in multiple places at once. In the lower portion of the drawing, a woman lies very still in bed with her eyes closed and her body connected to assorted IV bags and related hospital equipment. The woman's heavily shadowed form contrasts with the brightness of her face and the subtle layer of light that extends like an aura around the edges of her silhouette. The concrete, naturalistic details of the darkened hospital room anchor the work visually and conceptually, just as they ground the mystical component of the story. Reflecting these themes, the drawing's textured graphite surface displays gentle tonal modulations that create a subtle pathway of light that links the various registers of the composition. Floating directly above the woman's reclining body is a complementary image of her upright etheric form, which is seen from behind. While the shades are drawn in the woman's darkened hospital room, the ascending figure stands poised on the threshold of an open doorway that is made of light. The doorway seems to expand and tilt forward slightly, as if drawing nearer to meet her rising presence.

During our visit, this woman described her experience of love and light as a state of enlightenment. When the term is approached broadly, enlightenment signifies "the action of bringing someone to a state of greater knowledge, under-standing, or insight; the state of being enlightened in this way."[42] This woman's story is indeed a testament to her experience of what it is like to be part of an illuminated world. Notably, while she also mentioned her informal engagement with Tibetan Buddhism, her story does not reflect a traditional Buddhist conception of enlightenment (or nirvana) as "the state of spiritual insight or awareness which frees a person from the cycle of suffering and rebirth." This woman made no such claims to a universal knowledge or comprehensive understanding of the nature of reality. Moreover, her story was not about the extin-guishing of the self and its desires, nor did she offer any discussion of karma or the cycles of life, or any apprehension of the non-existence of the self.[43] Rather, her highly self-aware narrative was presented in very moving personal terms.

Notably, the esoteric tradition of *Dzogchen* yields a somewhat different understanding of the term "enlightenment" than that which is found in other Buddhist writings. In tantra, a key term is *chang chup sem* which, in Tibetan, refers to the mind of enlightenment. In this tradition enlightenment is seen as part of the nature of reality, and it reflects a sense of universal love. The mind (*sem*) of enlightenment represents a state of being that is purified and clarified of any darkness or limitation (*chang*), and is replete with a sense of spaciousness, a state of giving rise to everything and allowing it to flower up (*chup*). The mind of enlightenment thus reflects a state of transcendence and a realization of wisdom beyond the normative sense of the self.[44]

In turn, this woman had reached a place where she infused everything with love. And as she dissolved into a state of radiant love, reality responded around her and radiant love became her reality. This woman was extremely bright and intensely aware as she described a sense of liberation, oneness, and joy. As we sat together, both her spirit and her conscious personality appeared like rising light. It was clear that she not only felt the love of others, but that she experienced the exaltation of knowing herself as love, a state of being that she called "Enlightenment."

Figure 12. Lyn Smallwood, *They Were All Clapping for Me*, 2012, charcoal and pastel on white Canson paper, 12 x 9 in.

Chapter 10

Transcendence: The Doorway Between Heaven and Earth: They Were All Clapping for Me

"The hardest thing I've ever done in my entire life was coming back. If I have to make the choice again, I won't turn back this time."

These compelling words were spoken by a very unassuming, middle-aged man who told me an extraordinary story about his experience of the heaven world. When I initially introduced myself as an Artist In Residence and asked the man if he had a special image in his mind, he quickly responded, "You mean something like going to heaven and coming back to earth?" With a twinkle, I told him that would be just fine. The man went on to tell me that, several years prior, he had undergone a near-death experience.[45] His vivid account included a tunnel leading to white light, a sense of the beaming love he felt all around him, and his own sacrifice in returning to earth. Thus much like the young girl who envisioned herself being held in the palm of God's hands, or the woman who had entered a state that she called Enlightenment, this man's demeanor was gentle yet extremely clear and determined as he said, "I try to share my knowledge with other people, because I want others to know that there is a heaven."

As I stood in this man's room, he went into detail about his end of life event. He matter-of-factly told me that more than a decade ago he had died, gone to heaven, and returned home because of his concern for his young son. With a quiver in his voice, he said to me, "The hardest thing I've ever done in my entire life was coming back," and if he had to do it all over again, he wouldn't turn back a second time. Yet as difficult as it was to return, he affirmed that the love he experienced in heaven stayed with him up through the very moment of our visit. As he said, "All the time, I feel that love."

This man was only in early middle age when his near-death experience occurred, and it had a profound impact on the remainder of his life. Since that event, "Yes, I've changed my life. I live very carefully and try to cause no harm." During his life review session, he felt all the pain and suffering that he had caused in this lifetime, from early childhood onward. He also said that he feels "stronger and more powerful" because of this experience. Placing careful weight on the final words of his sentence, he emphasized, "I want others to know that there is a heaven," and he asked me to help share his story of the meeting place between worlds. His artwork is entitled,

They Were All Clapping for Me

My story is probably not dissimilar to many people's.
My son was very young,
And he didn't yet know the Lord,
Which is to say, he wasn't baptized.

One day I was with my father-in-law
And we were going camping.
I wasn't feeling very good, and I fainted.
I woke up on the floor,
And they took me to the hospital.
I was on the ER table,
And the next thing, I'm gone,
Dead on the table, with a completely blocked artery.
I saw two women, nurses, holding my hands,
And my father-in-law,
With his jaw dropped, looking down at me.

I had a time out.

In going through the doorway between heaven and earth,
I was reviewing my life
And I felt all the pain and suffering
Of each person I had hurt in my life.

I went to a tunnel,
And there was a beautiful, brilliant white light.
It's a glowing brilliant light,
So brilliant it almost made your eyes hurt.
I saw a beautiful lady,
And it was like we walked down a hallway,
And we walked through a pathway to get to a stadium.
There were people cheering for me and clapping.
The people looked like sparks of white light,
With splashes of multicolored, glimmering light inside of them.
They were all cheering and clapping,
And saying I was so great and wonderful.

The feeling I had was that of a mother
With her arms around a small child.
I was being held in love.
They all had their arms around me.
They told me I was going to stay there with them,
And I said no, I had to go back for my son,
So that he can know the Lord.
And they let me go back.

I never forgot that day.
I felt stronger and really empowered after that.
I tell people,
You have to have faith,
And you have to believe.

But I don't have to believe.
I have the knowledge.
All the time,
I feel that love.

In Lyn Smallwood's drawing (Figure 12), two figures walk together along a bright pathway toward the end of a dark tunnel. The figures are poised on the threshold of an open doorway, out of which streams brilliant white light. The man and his guide are about to enter a stadium filled with luminous people who are all cheering for him. Playing on degrees of abstraction, in this elegant drawing the figures' single, merged shadow on the ground below loosely resembles an angel's wing. In this spare scene, the figures have form and substance even as they remain hazy and translucent. Throughout the drawing, modulated tonal gradations of black and white create a radiant *and* a radiating space in which dark walls project backward and bright light projects forward. The textured ground of the white Canson laid paper provides an underlying grid or matrix to hold the etheric charcoal and pastel forms. These delicate, chalky materials constitute the expressive foundation that supports the possibility of visibly representing otherwise invisible presences. Much like the man's narrative, this imagery exceeds the boundaries of representation, even as it suggests a glimpse of a transcendent world that lies beyond. Thus throughout this minimalist artwork, we are seeing what we can't see.

Such an aesthetic approach represents an apt metaphor for near-death experience itself. Like many people who have undergone such an experience, this man characterized this encounter as a life-changing and life-affirming event. The experience trans-formed his understanding of the relationship between the material and the metaphysical worlds. In turn, this is a story of transcendence because it exceeds the limits of the material world as it presents imagery that climbs across the familiar terrain of knowledge and experience to enter a numinous domain of continuing life.

When engaging these subjects both inside and outside of the hospital, I have repeatedly witnessed the ways in which death represents a capital fear of many people, primarily because they cannot imagine the continuation of life beyond the death of the physical body. This concern relates directly to how we imagine the relationship between the material and the metaphysical domains. Regarding these subjects, the scholar Allan Kellehear has traced several themes associated with death and dying in the social science and behavioral studies literatures. While there is not a consensus regarding the experience of dying, Kellehear has identified seven key themes that recur in these texts. They include issues of agency and control; linearity and rites of passage; oscillation and intermittent periods of decline and improvement; states of disengagement and withdrawal; the disintegration of the physical body; the disenfranchisement associated with the segregation of the dying; and finally, transcendence, where dying is seen as a transformational event. Notably, the theme of transcendence is primarily associated with the phenomena of near-death experiences and related deathbed visions.[46]

Much like the man whose story is recounted in this chapter, the love stories that appear in *The Heart of the Hereafter* can help to expand our understanding of the various types of transcendence that arise at the end of life. In so doing, these delicate yet powerful artworks hold the potential to broaden and transform both our practices and our perspectives concerning issues of transcendence. Notably, these themes also relate closely to the opening image of the woman whose room was filled with the sweet scent of rose petals, and to the epigraph with which I began this book: "And the glorious beauty shall be a fading flower" (Isaiah 28.4). So often when we approach end of life

issues, we immediately think of ugliness and despair, disintegration and dissolution. Yet much like this biblical quotation, the
stories contained in this volume provide alternative perspectives
on life and the end of life, a complex interplay in which states of
deterioration and ecstasy are folded together as one. In the
decline of the fading flower, it is indeed possible to witness a
vision of glorious beauty.

Moreover, as is the case with so many reports of near-death
experiences, the man whose story appears here described how
part of his transition entailed a life review session. As he stepped
into the light, he entered into a heavenly realm that encompassed
everything, just as he experienced a session in which nothing was
lost or forgotten. In philosophical terms, this portion of the man's
near-death experience bridged the gap between ethics and
transcendence. That is, the man gained extreme clarity and
insight regarding the consequences of his words and actions, and
how they effected or harmed others. He understood the wrong-
doing of taking away another person's strong sense of well-being,
and the corresponding need to practice due diligence toward
everyone at all times. Through his experiences with individuals
in his lifetime, the man gained insight into a broader set of values
and principles that taught him to assume a greater sense of
responsibility and to recognize what we all have in common.
Thus much like the opening story of the teacher who changed her
students' lives as she taught them how to read, this man experienced a similar lack of conflict regarding being in service to
himself, to those around him, and to a higher power. These
powerful life lessons immediately preceded his encounter with
divine presences. Implicitly referring to angelic forms and to the
spirits of family members waiting to greet loved ones, this man
described being accompanied by a beautiful lady, and walking
into a stadium and seeing people who resembled sparks of bright
white light with splashes of multicolored light gleaming inside of
them. As they all cheered for him, they affirmed his sense of

being held in love, much like the young girl who described herself as being held *In the Palm of God's Hands*. This transcendent experience showed the man that, when we leave, we take the most of us with ourselves, and the best of us with ourselves.

When this man returned to his life, he had the strength to live differently because he had direct knowledge of ever-beingness, divine love, and the state of grace. This experience created a deep sense of peace and non-questioned belief. And this sense of the continuation of life in the afterlife changed his state of mind and body, both in his life and now at the end of his life, once again.

As he said, "All the time, I feel that love."

Afterword

Philosophy: A Life Review for the Living

So many times, I will be out walking somewhere and I'll run into a colleague or an acquaintance, and they will ask me about my teaching and how my work is going. I can hear myself responding enthusiastically, "Things are great, just great. I'm teaching a seminar on the end of life, and I've got a whole room full of pre-meds and humanities students. I'm also working with people at the end of life, terminal cancer patients at M. D. Anderson, and it's just amazing. I love doing this work." People will often hear these words and—with varying degrees of tact—they will look at me like I've completely gone out of my mind. In their own minds, they will only have heard the words "end of life" and "terminal cancer," and they will be stopped cold. What they will not have recognized is the unbelievable love that comes through each week, which I have been privileged to witness and experience on so many occasions. Thus the reason why people are so amazed is because, in their own minds, they could not possibly imagine doing this work and having such experiences themselves. Sometimes the gap feels nearly unbridgeable between what the other person is hearing and feeling, and the sense of absolute joy and spiritual wonder and gratitude that I feel, both in the hospital room and throughout the writing of this book.

Red Roses and Ivy: Translational Empathy

One day I met an older man who was about to leave for hospice, and whose journey now was all about pain management. As we talked, I learned that this creative man was an artist, a gardener, and a cook. He described how his creativity was connected to his deep sense of spirituality, and how this had once saved his life. At one point, he became so depressed with his cancer diagnosis that he contemplated suicide, but then he decided against it. He told me that he started walking out into the ocean, and when he was in beyond his knees, he heard someone call his name. He looked back at the sea wall, but no one was standing there, so he knew he had to turn back. That experience made him realize that it was not yet his time, and suicide was not for him. As he told me, "You have to have faith. You have to live." He also emphasized that he now shares this message with others who are suffering. Thus applying the lessons of his own experience to his later outreach efforts with people in similar circumstances, this man transformed his own pain into what might be called gestures of translational empathy.

For this man, red roses and ivy served as intertwined symbols of the passion for life and the freedom of living. In the handmade paper journal, this man drew an image of a heart surrounded by an open red rose, which was then surrounded by sprigs of flowing green ivy. The man himself appeared to be drawing breath as he drew the deep green leaves and stems of the plants. As our visit unfolded, the composition formed a bouquet, which also appeared as a symbolic self-portrait:

Red Roses and Ivy

Ivy.
I love ivy.
I used to have ivies growing all over,
Especially all around my front door.
I love to be outside.
My favorite place is my own yard.

When I think about ivy,
I feel free.
Ivy is so free, and I love to see it grow.
When I think about ivy,

I don't think about anything else
But freedom.

I also love roses, red roses.
I think about love when I think about red roses.
I love to see the flowers and plants grow.
They open up my lungs.
I feel at ease when I'm around plants like that.

Ivy is so fresh and free.
It's free to expand,
And it's free to grow everywhere.

I Couldn't Believe I Did That

When I first started doing this clinical work, I had two primary fears. Initially, I was afraid that I would see something in the medical context that would be so disturbing that I would have to turn away and leave the room. I was also concerned that I would not be good enough to do this work, and that I would have nothing of value to offer the patients. Fortunately, those fears were dispelled after my second week of work. At that point I knew that it was not just a fluke and that, even though I had not officially worked in a hospital or hospice before—and so, in one sense, I didn't actually know what I was doing—that somehow, I just deeply knew what I was doing. Paradoxically, even though I didn't know, I already knew. And just as this work lends itself to a new discourse in the medical humanities, it also reflects an age-old tradition of care giving.[47] These paradoxes are very beautiful, and they relate closely to the creative practices of being open to the open, and of holding on by letting go. These themes thread through the work in the hospital room, the writing of this book, and (end of) life experience itself. Taken together, they create a radiant space that is filled with love, joy, and wonder.

One day on the ward I met a middle-aged woman who was struggling—physically, emotionally, and spiritually—with her advanced ovarian cancer and impending death. Although she had limited formal education, this woman was very smart and very poised, and she had a special talent for working with her hands. She told me how much she loved to sew, crochet, and decorate cakes. As we flipped through a garden catalogue together, this soft-spoken woman told me that, above all, "flowers are my passion."

In her artwork, flowers vibrantly bridged the domains of the decorative and the numinous as they appeared in the home and the church, spaces of domestic warmth and sacramental ritual. As objects of beauty, joy, comfort, and ceremony, flowers provided a tangible means for this woman to gain self-knowledge and self-confidence as she recognized her own creative accomplishments:

I Couldn't Believe I Did That

My image is of a bouquet of flowers.
No matter what flowers you look at,
They're all so beautiful.

I love to do flower arrangements.
That's my passion.
I like all the flowers
But I love the roses.
I had a business out of my home,
And I would do flower arrangements for proms, funerals, and
*   weddings.*
I'm a crafty person,
And I love working with my hands.
Once I made some arrangements for a wedding.
The baskets of flowers were pink, gold, and white,

Filled with daisies, gladiolas, and roses.
At the church, the baskets stood at the two sides of the altar,
With the white candles burning on either side.

It was really pretty,
And I was so proud.
I couldn't believe I did that.

Within the poetic imagery of palliative care—as within life itself—there are many scenes of gardens, sanctuaries, and vibrant living presences. Each one is unique, and each one is beautiful. Just as the imagery of gardens and flowers frequently crosses the boundaries between the sacred and the profane, the artworks express people's profound sense of identification with a beauty that simultaneously encompasses and transcends the self.

And the glorious beauty shall be a fading flower.

It is my hope that by reading *The Heart of the Hereafter* and allowing the artworks to touch your own heart and mind that you too will feel a sense of this love, this joy, and this wonder. In this way, this book can help to serve as a life review for the living. The same types of love that appear throughout this volume are found everywhere in life itself. This love is in your life just as much as it is in mine and in the lives of the people whose stories I share. Perhaps the differential is that the end of life represents a critical juncture that allows us to feel the extraordinary intensity of the love that is in you and in me and in everyone. In all instances, the key is to look for the love, to be open to whatever form it takes, and to express gratitude for whatever arises. Such love both touches and transcends our lives, just as it seems to continue with a life and a power all its own.

This love is a blessing to you, and to me, and to all of us.

Illustrations

Figure 10   Lyn Smallwood, *Our Hearts are the Same*, 2012, charcoal and pastel on white Canson paper, 12 1/8 x 9 in.

Figure 11   Lyn Smallwood, *I'm Calling It Enlightenment*, 2013, graphite on Arches paper, 9 5/8 x 9 in.

Figure 12   Lyn Smallwood, *They Were All Clapping for Me*, 2012, charcoal and pastel on white Canson paper, 12 x 9 in.

Notes

1   Anna-Leila Williams, "Perspectives on spirituality at the end of life: A meta-summary," *Palliative and Supportive Care* 4 (2006), p. 416.

2   In a study of "Spirituality, Religiosity, and Spiritual Pain in Advanced Cancer Patients" conducted in the Department of Palliative Care at M. D. Anderson, one hundred patients were interviewed in the Palliative Care outpatient clinic. Of this sample, 88 of the 100 participants self-reported their religious belief or affiliation as being Christian, of which 80 characterized themselves as Protestant and 8 as Roman Catholic. The remaining individuals identified themselves as being Jewish (4), atheist (4), Buddhist (2), Muslim (1), and Other (1). See Marvin O. Delgado Guay et al., "Spirituality, Religiosity, and Spiritual Pain in Advanced Cancer Patients," *Journal of Pain and Symptom Management* 41 (no. 6, June 2011), pp. 986-94.

3   Regarding the ethical, scientific, practical, and theological difficulties that can arise from clinical associations of medicine and religion, and the cautions that should be exercised accordingly, see Richard P. Sloan, *Blind Faith: The Unholy Alliance of Religion and Medicine* (New York: St. Martin's, 2006).

4   My monograph, *Words Beyond Words: Finding Language at the End of Life*, is forthcoming from Intellect Books, U.K. in association with the University of Chicago Press.

5   The illustrations included here are facsimile reproductions of a fifteenth-century volume housed in the British Museum, as presented in W. Harry Rylands, ed., *The Ars Moriendi: A reprint in facsimile of a treatise spekynge of the arte & crafte to knowe well to dye* (London: Wyman & Sons, 1881).

6   For a discussion that locates the *ars moriendi* within a

broader historical analysis of the imagery of death and dying, see Philippe Ariès's magisterial study, *Images of Man and Death*, trans. Janet Lloyd (Cambridge: Harvard University Press, 1985), pp. 147-53. Ariès's text includes five illustrations from a fifteenth-century *Ars Moriendi* in the Bibliothèque des Arts Décoratifs, Paris.

7 This phrase was offered by my student, Sarah Long.

8 See Gary L. Ebersole's essay on "Death" in Lindsay Jones, ed., *Encyclopedia of Religion*, vol. 4 (Detroit: Macmillan Reference, 2005), pp. 2235-2245. In this entry, Ebersole notes that images of death have also been used to educate and control populations by promoting sanctioned behaviors while creating fear around other, less desirable ones. Perhaps most intriguing is the insight that "the manner in which death and afterlife (or, the different consequences of death) are imagined and represented informs the lived experiences of death both by the dying person and the survivors." For thoughtful discussions of end of life rituals associated with various faith traditions, see Harold Coward and Kelli I. Stajduhar, eds., *Religious Understandings of a Good Death in Hospice Palliative Care* (Albany: SUNY Press, 2012).

9 For an incisive critique of the *ars moriendi* tradition and a discussion of competing, contemporary scripts for dying, see James W. Green, *Beyond the Good Death: The Anthropology of Modern Dying* (Philadelphia: University of Pennsylvania Press, 2008). In this volume, Green offers critical commentary regarding the "personalized and positive" narratives of the "good death" that are popular today, which range from specialized conceptions of death for niche audiences to the stage model that Elisabeth Kübler-Ross pioneered in *On Death and Dying* (1969). As Green notes, "This model of a systematic, gentle, peaceful resolve into death is one modern *ars moriendi*, and it has had a powerful impact." Yet as Green points out, Kübler-Ross's discussion is

problematic in that it offers a normative, universalizing model of death that was based on the progression of chronic disease among a white, middle class population. As Green candidly states, "the rhetoric of 'good death' and 'death-denial' may be more a matter of powerful institutional agendas for the efficient management of dying people than of individual preferences." Thus for Green and other critical commentators, the *ars moriendi* traditions are associated with theological and thanatological metanarratives that remain inextricably connected to particular bases of social and institutional power. Regarding these subjects, see especially pp. 8-11 and 188 of Green's volume.

10 Atul Gawande, "Letting Go: What should medicine do when it can't save your life?" *New Yorker* (Aug. 2, 2010), accessed online at http://www.newyorker.com/reporting/2010/08/02/100802fa_fact_gawande?printable=true

11 I am grateful to Sally Huang for her thoughtful comments concerning the challenges that future generations of healthcare providers will face.

12 On these subjects, see also *"Ars Vivendi*: The Art of Dying Teaches Us the Art of Living" in Virginia Morris, *Talking About Death* (Chapel Hill: Algonquin Books, 2004), pp. 251-57.

13 David Morgan, *Visual Piety: A History and Theory of Popular Religious Images* (Berkeley: University of California Press, 1998), pp. 9-10.

14 James Faubion's insightful comments helped to clarify and shape the character of this discussion.

15 The artworks that appear in this text were not produced *in situ* at the patient's bedside or from a photograph or any other type of derivative material. The images contain no recognizable likenesses that bear any resemblance to any individuals with whom I have worked, nor do they resemble any visual artworks now in the possession of surviving

family members. All names have been changed to preserve the privacy of the individuals involved. The artworks thus comply with the standards associated with patient privacy and confidentiality. In addition, this project has been favorably reviewed by two independent Institutional Review Boards (IRBs) at Rice University and at the M. D. Anderson Cancer Center. Notably, the subjects of this project are universal, human, and deeply important; as such, they raise a host of compelling issues regarding subjectivity, sensitivity, visibility, representation, and compassion that must be processed within our culture. At the same time, due to privacy concerns, the narratives presented here are neces-sarily abstracted sketches that are intended to be generic and anonymous. Particular identifying details relating to specific individuals have been omitted or altered, thereby assuring HIPPA compliance and preserving issues of confidentiality, particularly as specified under "The Privacy Rule," The Belmont Report, and the Department of Health and Human Services Office for Human Research Protections, including The Common Rule and subparts B, C, and D of the Health and Human Services specifications as outlined in the Code of Federal Regulations (CFR) at 45 CFR 164 and 165, which specifies the "safe harbor" method of de-identification. Finally, it should be emphasized that the artworks are not presented as sentimental fictions intended to romanticize the end of life or to support a larger cultural narrative regarding what it might mean to "die a good death." Some of the stories represent condensations of two or more patient encounters in which closely related narratives emerged during the visits. All of the events I describe actually occurred, and the words are the patients' own.

16　See the entry on "philanthropy" in the *Oxford English Dictionary*, 2nd ed. (Oxford: Clarendon Press, 1989), accessed online　at

http://www.oed.com.ezproxy.rice.edu/view/Entry/142408?re
directedFrom=philanthropy#eidAll future references will be
to this edition of the *OED*.

17   Ian Jacobster offered these reflections in his essay, "Talking
About Love: A Dinner Conversation," December 2013.

18   Like many of the stories that appear in this volume, this
narrative may raise questions regarding the extent to which
the production of the artworks is influenced by the palliative
medications administered at the end of life, and if so, what
role these drugs might play in producing the sometimes
extraordinary states of consciousness that become reflected
in the narratives. When I put this question directly to
palliative care physicians, they responded that, while drug
interactions are variable with each patient, the medications
do not in fact interfere with a person's thought processes.
The exception would be in cases of delirium, where the
medications would be evident; and when palliative medications are not in balance, a person can be sleepy or slowed
down. (Delirium is a condition that affects cognitive
function, and in Palliative Medicine the neuroleptic dose is
regulated by several factors, including the person's disorien-
tation to time and place, agitation, hallucinations, and
delusions.) Regarding the production of the artworks, the
doctors expressed their sense that people are not speaking
from a drug-inflected state produced by the psychopharma-
cology of pain treatment. Regarding issues of cognitive
impairment in general, it is the physicians' sense that,
because a person is on opioids does not mean that they are
without capacity or competency. As one physician put it,
"Drugs do not speak. People do. And in the artworks, they
are speaking from the heart." I am particularly grateful to
Drs. Donna Zhukovsky and Karen Cottingham for sharing
their thoughts on these subjects. For additional discussions
of the significant differences between drug-induced halluci-

nations and end of life visions, see Peter and Elizabeth Fenwick's study *The Art of Dying: A Journey to Elsewhere* (London: Continuum, 2008).

19 Notably, Artists In Residence are neither therapists nor art therapists. While the patient interactions often contain important psychodynamic insights and revelations, these activities represent not a therapy, but a critical intervention that broadly allows for the expression of personal uniqueness. Regarding some of the overlapping psychosocial and support functions that artistic activities can provide within an interdisciplinary team, see the section on "Art Therapy" in Max Watson et al., *The Oxford Handbook of Palliative Care*, 2nd ed. (Oxford: Oxford University Press, 2009), pp. 803-804. For a clinical discussion of related concepts, see Mélanie Vachon et al., "A Conceptual Analysis of Spirituality at the End of Life," *Journal of Palliative Medicine* 12 (2009), pp. 53-59.

20 During 2012 and 2013, various members of the palliative care interdisciplinary team presented this case under the title "Hoka Hey! It is a Good Day to Live: Relieving Physical, Emotional, and Spiritual Suffering of Persons with Advanced Illness and their Caregivers." These public presentations included the Grand Rounds Lecture in Psychosocial Medicine (April 10, 2012); the Texas Medical Center's Quarterly Pain and Palliative Care Grand Rounds Lecture (February 7, 2013); and the conference session "A Humanitarian Approach to Psychosocial Suffering Influencing the Experience of Disease" at The Collective Soul Symposium: Relieving Physical, Emotional, and Spiritual Suffering of Persons With Advanced Illness and their Caregivers (January 20, 2012).

21 Saunders also discussed the pain experienced by the medical staff, and their corresponding need for support at the professional level. See Cicely Saunders et al., "Other Components

of Total Pain" in *Living with Dying: A Guide to Palliative Care,* 3rd ed. (Oxford: Oxford University Press, 1995), pp. 45-58. For a description of St. Christopher's Hospice, which Saunders founded, see Shirley du Boulay, *Changing the Face of Death: The Story of Cicely Saunders* (Norfolk, U.K.: Religious and Moral Education Press, 2001). In my academic writings and teaching, I reflect on the various ways in which the humanities can contribute to addressing human suffering within a medical context which, in turn, can help to shape an overall model of care.

22 This insight on *amour propre* was expressed by Jose Chapa in his play, *Memoirs of an Actor: The Truth in Hiding and Hiding in the Truth,* November 2013.

23 I am grateful to Elitza Ranova for her insightful comments concerning the life-changing effects of narratives and their potential impact on subtle states of bodily presence.

24 According to the *Oxford English Dictionary,* agape is "the communal religious meal believed to have been held in the early Church in close relation to the Eucharist" and thus is a "love-feast." See the entry on "agape" in the *Oxford English Dictionary,* accessed online at http://www.oed.com.ezp roxy.rice.edu/search?searchType=dictionary&q=agape&_sea rchBtn=Search

25 The concept of "social death" reflects the various forms of physical and emotional separation and rejection that a person may experience at the end of life. For a discussion of "the theme of disengagement: dying as withdrawal" and a summary of the complex writings on this subject, see Allan Kellehear, "What the social and behavioural studies say about dying" in *The Study of Dying: From Autonomy to Transformation,* ed. Allan Kellehear (Cambridge: Cambridge University Press, 2009), pp. 8-12.

26 A condensed version of this story appears in my book *The Angels In Between: The Book of Muse* (Winchester, U.K: Axis

Mundi Books, 2013), pp. 175-76.

27 Jean-Luc Nancy, *God, Justice, Love, Beauty: Four Little Dialogues*, trans. Sarah Clift (New York: Fordham University Press, 2011), p. 75.

28 C. S. Lewis, *The Four Loves* (1960; New York: Harcourt Brace, 1988), ch. 5.

29 Sigmund Freud, *Civilization and Its Discontents*, trans. and ed. James Strachey (1930; New York: W. W. Norton, 1961), p. 13. Eros represents a particularly complex concept in Freudian psychology, as does the complementary conception of thanatos, or the death drive. In his writings, Freud identified the two drives as fundamental structures within the human psyche that represent the impulses of life and death, respectively. Freud characterized eros as an energetic force that is associated with sexual pleasure and passion, the impulse toward self-preservation, and the continuation of life itself. In contrast, thanatos is seen as a destructive impulse associated with the instinct for death, and it can include expressions of pain, aggression, and violence, all of which can extend toward the annihilation of oneself or others. Presented in such dialogical terms, eros and thanatos often emerge as dualistic structures. Yet Freud saw the conflict between these impulses as central to a developmental struggle within the evolution of human civilization, and he noted the ways in which these two seemingly oppositional impulses sometimes became coextensively expressed in sadism and masochism.

30 For a suggestive discussion of the ways in which love can appear to suspend time when placed within artistic and cinematic contexts, see Alexander Nemerov, *Wartime Kiss: Visions of the Moment in the 1940s* (Princeton: Princeton University Press, 2013).

31 Regarding storge, see the discussion of "Affection" in chapter three of Lewis's *The Four Loves*, and the entry on the term in

the *Oxford English Dictionary*, accessed online at http://www.oed.com.ezproxy.rice.edu/view/Entry/190941?re directedFrom=storge&

32 See the definition of "theophany" in the *Oxford English Dictionary*, accessed online at http://www.oed.com.ezproxy .rice.edu/view/Entry/200402?redirectedFrom=theophany&.

33 The primary entry on "grace" (as a noun) in the *Oxford English Dictionary* is voluminous and fascinating. Among the numerous definitions of "grace," the *OED* notes that the term is also used in scriptural and theological language to connote the favor of God with regard to salvation and blessings. See the entry on "grace" in the *Oxford English Dictionary*, accessed online at: http://www.oed.com.ez proxy.rice.edu/view/Entry/80373?rskey=i4Ujja&result=1&is Advanced=false#eid

34 Regarding the conception of God as the "ground of all being," see especially the opening pages of volume two of Paul Tillich's *Systematic Theology: Three Volumes in One* (Chicago: University of Chicago Press, 1967).

35 Regarding the resonance of this story with themes of social justice, see my article "Four Butterflies: End of Life Stories of Transition and Transformation," *Pastoral Psychology* 62 (no. 2, 2013), pp. 133-49.

36 See the definitions of "caritas" and "charity" in the *Oxford English Dictionary*, accessed online at http://www.oed.com. ezproxy.rice.edu/view/Entry/27999?redirectedFrom=caritas & and http://www.oed.com.ezproxy.rice.edu/view/Entry/ 30731?redirectedFrom=charity&

37 C. S. Lewis's extended discussion of charity appears as the final chapter of *The Four Loves*. As Lewis presciently notes, it is more difficult to receive the love of charity than to give it.

38 See the definition of "forgiveness" in the *Oxford English Dictionary*, accessed online at http://www.oed.com.ezp roxy.rice.edu/viewdictionaryentry/Entry/73337

39 Regarding the various ways in which religious systems can provide a framework for creating relationships between human beings and sacred figures, as well as promoting understandings of the connections between worlds, see Robert A. Orsi, *Between Heaven and Earth: The Religious Worlds People Make and the Scholars Who Study Them* (Princeton: Princeton University Press, 2005).

40 See the definition of "Gethsemane" in *Webster's Seventh New Collegiate Dictionary* (Springfield, MA: G. & C. Merriam, 1969), p. 351.

41 Lewis, *The Four Loves*, p. 6.

42 See the definitions of "enlightenment" and "nirvana" in the *Oxford English Dictionary*, accessed online at http://www.oed.com.ezproxy.rice.edu/view/Entry/62448?red irectedFrom=enlightenment#eid and http://www.oed.com.ez proxy.rice.edu/view/Entry/127265?redirectedFrom=nirvana# eid.

43 For an extended discussion of the various theological conno- tations of Enlightenment, particularly with regard to Asian religious traditions, see William K. Mahony's entry on "Enlightenment" in the *Encyclopedia of Religion*, vol. 4, p. 2792-2795. In particular, Mahony notes that "In the context of Asian religious traditions, especially of Buddhism, what is often translated as *enlightenment* typically refers to that existentially transformative experience in which one reaches complete and thorough understanding of the nature of reality and gains control over those psychic proclivities that determine the apparent structures and dynamics of the world. As is consistent with a general South and East Asian notion that final truth is apprehended through extraordinary 'sight', religious 'insight' or 'vision', enlightenment is often depicted as an experience in which one is said to 'see' things as they really are rather than as they merely appear to be." Moreover, this woman's story also reflects aspects of satori, a

conception of spiritual awakening in the Zen Buddhist tradition that is associated with "a sudden indescribable and uncommunicable inner experience of enlightenment." Yet while the *Oxford English Dictionary* definition of "satori" indicates that this state arrives suddenly and cannot be communicated, this woman's sense of enlightenment came at the end of her life and, by saying that she did not know what to call it, she communicated her experience very effectively. See the definition of "satori" in the *Oxford English Dictionary*, accessed online at http://www.oed.com.ezproxy.rice.edu/view/Entry/171245?redirectedFrom=satori#eid

44 I am grateful to my colleague Anne Klein for her comments on the various dimensions and resonances of the term "enlightenment" within the esoteric tradition. As she has observed, "The mind of enlightenment, unbounded wholeness, then, is a state of self-arisen wisdom, an open awareness united with clarity. Being all inclusive, it has no match, no pair, so it cannot be two; yet it is not only one, since it is the potential of all that exists." See Anne Carolyn Klein and Geshe Tenzin Wangyal Rinpoche, *Unbounded Wholeness: Dzogchen, Bon, and the Logic of the Nonconceptual* (New York: Oxford University Press, 2006), p. 57.

45 For a summary of the extensive literature on near-death experiences, see especially Bruce Greyson, "Near-death experiences and deathbed visions" in Kellehear, *The Study of Dying*, pp. 253-75. In this essay, Greyson provides a succinct and insightful analysis of the phenomenon of the near-death experience as a kind of "pseudo death," as well as the subsequent effects that such an experience can exert within an individual's network of personal and social relations. Drawing on Raymond Moody's foundational work, Greyson characterizes the near-death experience as being ineffable, peaceful, transient, and disembodied, as people describe meeting nonphysical beings of light, undergoing a life

review, encountering border points between worlds, and living their lives differently upon their return to earth. Such critical differentials can include a person's receiving knowledge that is not acquired through normal perception, as well as their experiencing a heightened state of awareness and mystical joy. In addition to Greyson, in *The Art of Dying: A Journey to Elsewhere*, Peter and Elizabeth Fenwick provide a valuable extended discussion of this phenomenon, including its problematic status within traditional biomedicine, as well as related empirical and symbolic accounts of dying, death, and near-death experiences. Their text also includes thoughtful analyses of transitional figures and their positive somatic effects. By expressing the sense that an extended mind is manifesting at the time of death, the Fenwicks' discussion broaches the space between biomedicine and consciousness studies.

46 See Kellehear, "What the social and behavioural studies say about dying," pp. 1-26.

47 I am grateful to N. J. Pierce for her insightful observations on this issue.

AXIS MUNDI
BOOKS

Axis Mundi Books provide the most revealing and coherent explorations and investigations of the world of hidden or forbidden knowledge. Take a fascinating journey into the realm of Esoteric Mysteries, Magic, Mysticism, Angels, Cosmology, Alchemy, Gnosticism, Theosophy, Kabbalah, Secret Societies and Religions, Symbolism, Quantum Theory, Apocalyptic Mythology, Holy Grail and Alternative Views of Mainstream Religion.